.

Feathered Critter Friends Vol. II

Feathered Critter Friends Vol. II

Rob Benton

ESOTERICOM®

ISBN 978-0-9980682-0-6

All birds depicted herein were photographed in the course of their natural behavior.
No bird was enticed, confined, entrapped, or harassed in any way
in the making of these photographs.

Captions indicate general identification of the bird
and where photograph was made.

Front cover: Crimson Sunbird, Singapore
Back cover: Common Hoopoe, Kanchanaburi, Thailand

So God created the great Sea Monsters
and every living Creature That moves,
with which the waters swarm,
according to their kinds,
and every winged bird according to its kind.
And God saw
that it was good.

And God blessed them, saying, "Be fruitful
and multiply on the earth."

Genesis 1: 21-22

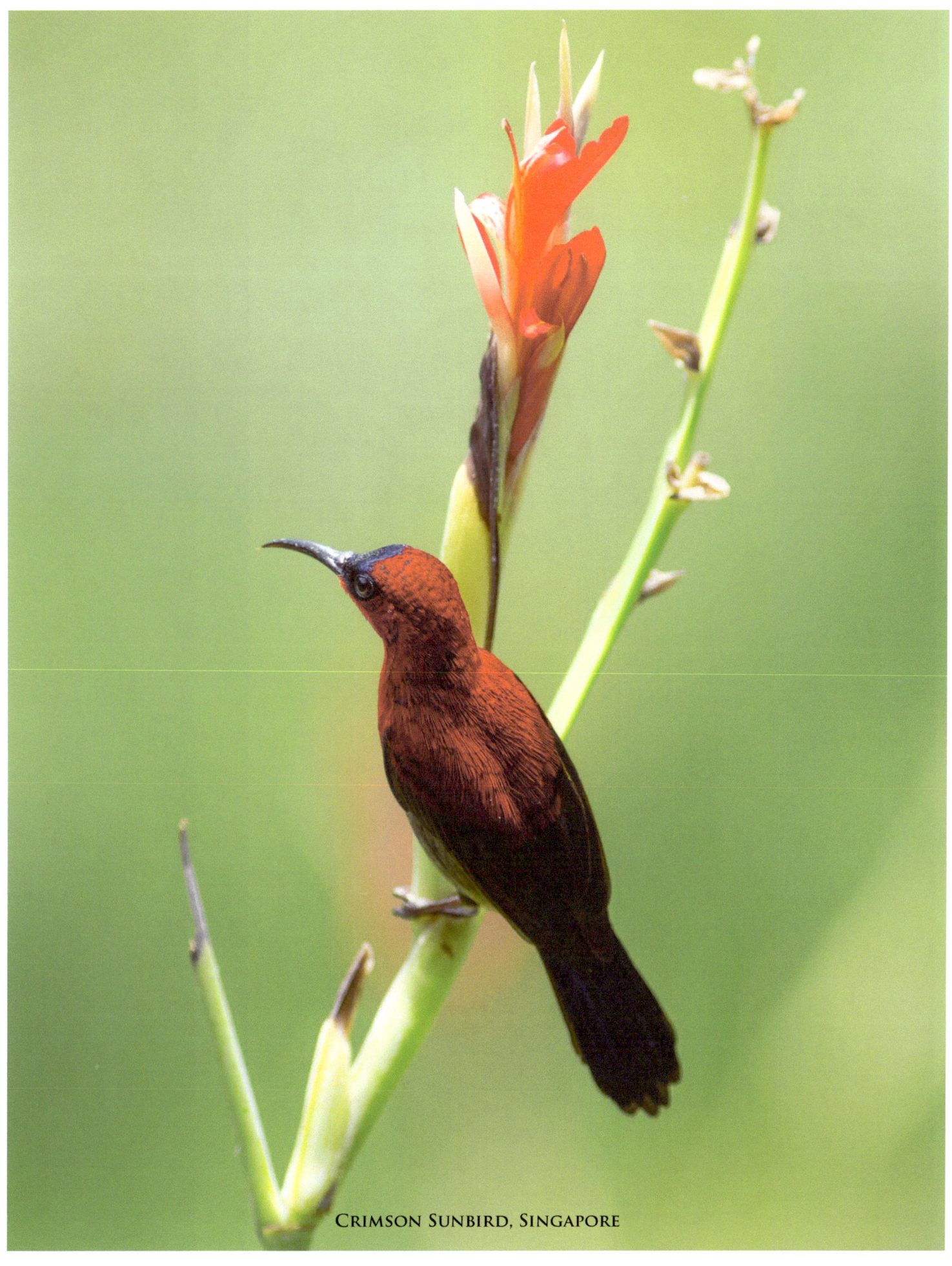

CRIMSON SUNBIRD, SINGAPORE

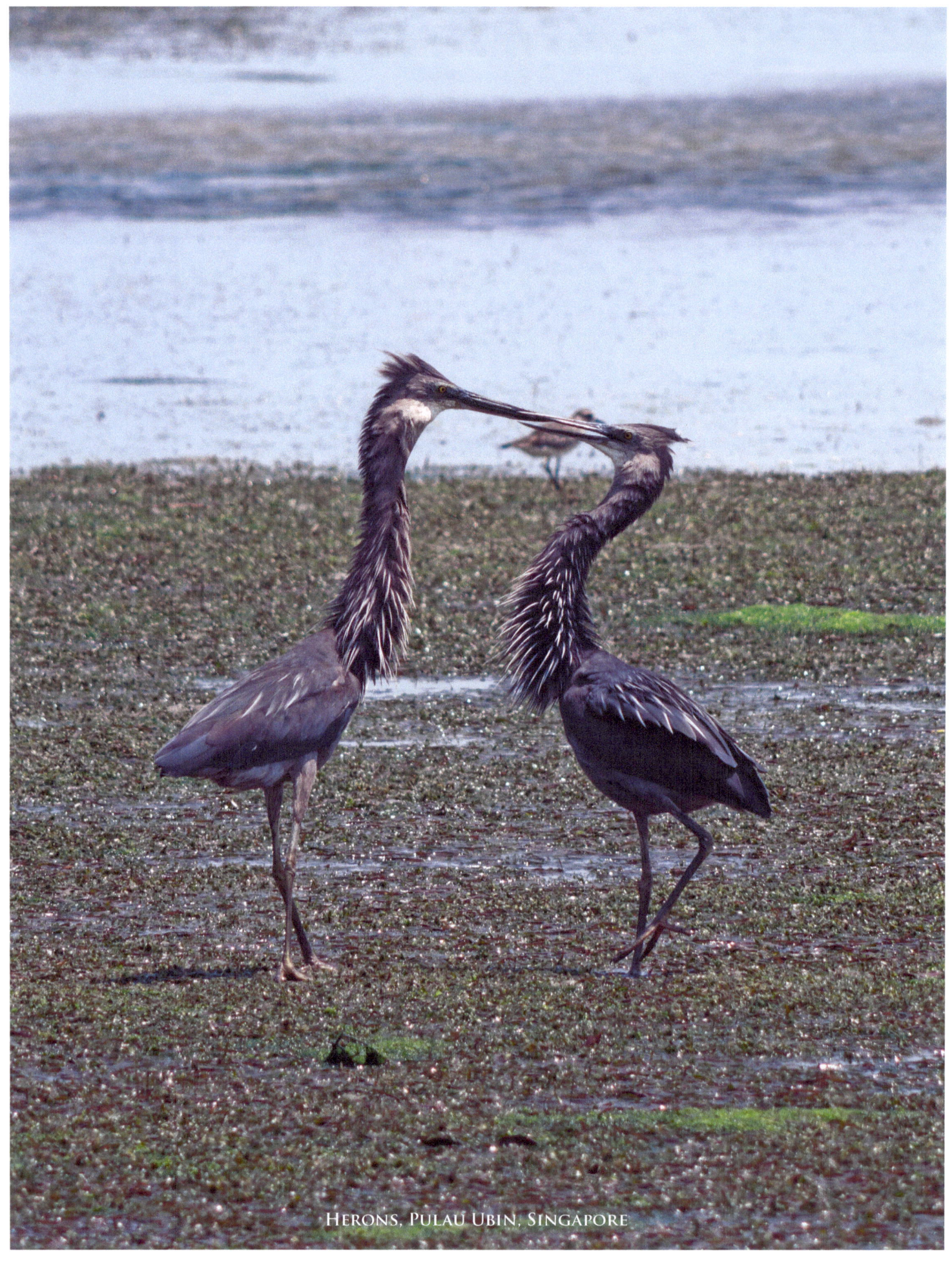

HERONS, PULAU UBIN, SINGAPORE

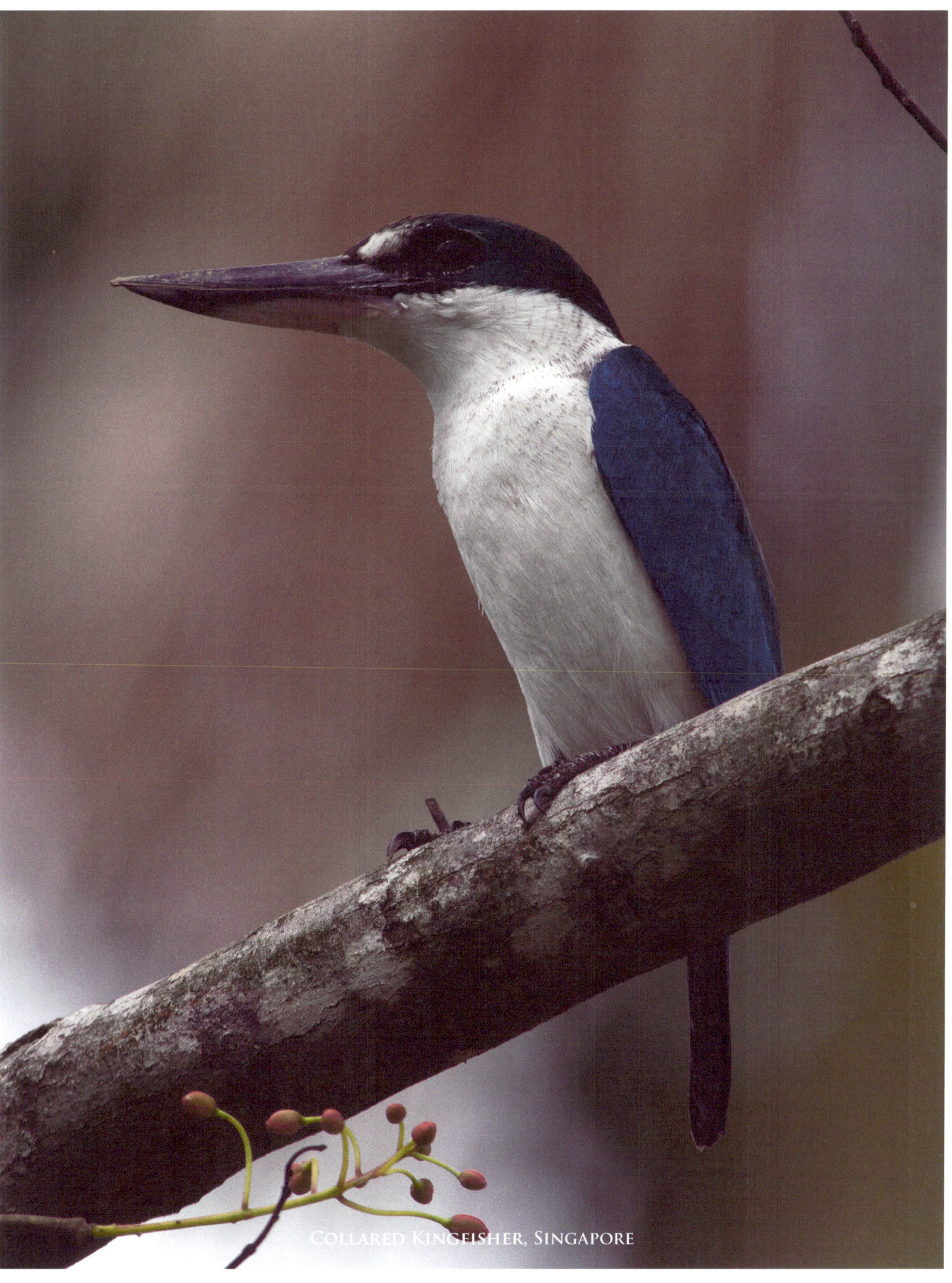

COLLARED KINGFISHER, SINGAPORE

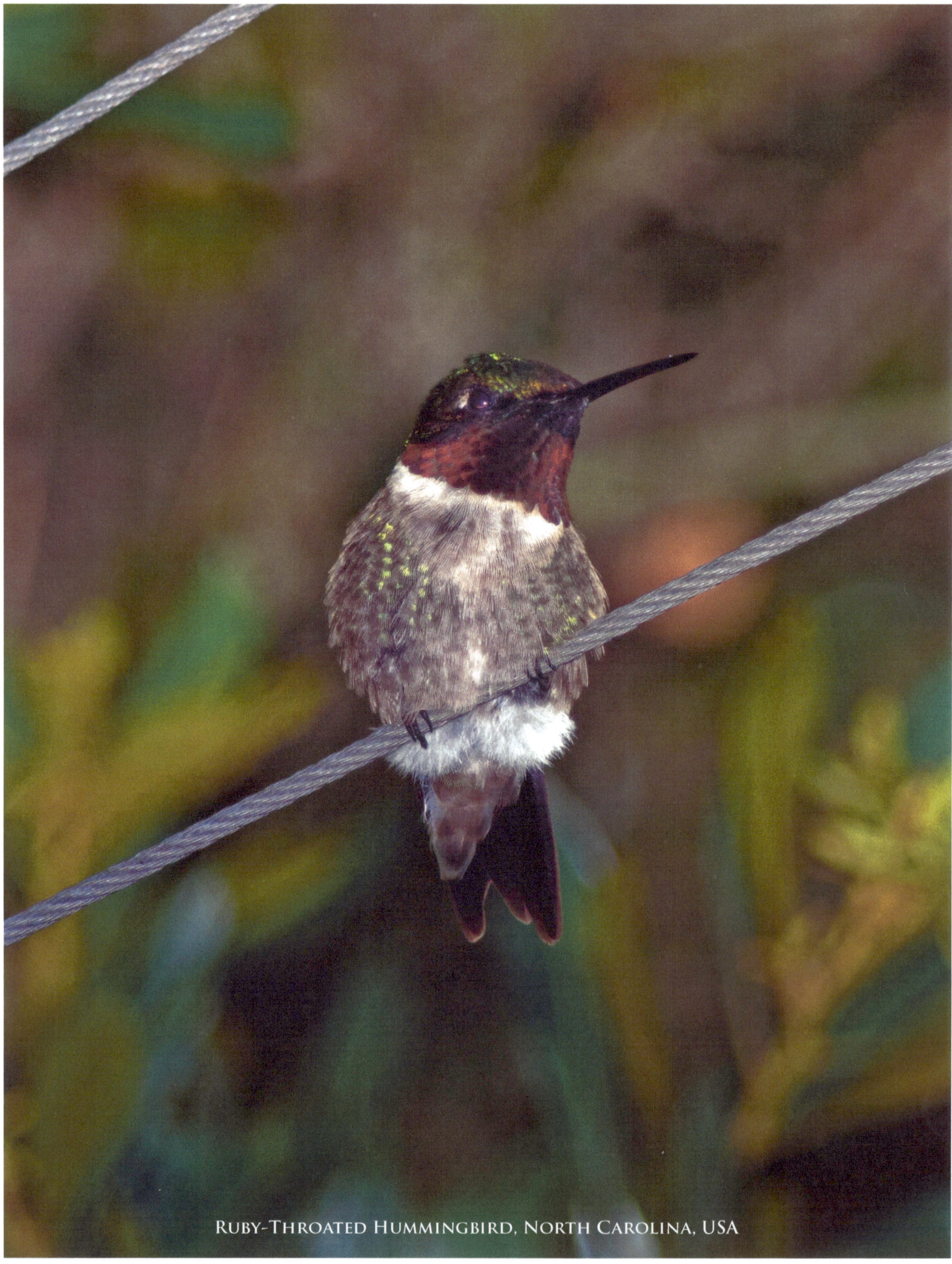

RUBY-THROATED HUMMINGBIRD, NORTH CAROLINA, USA

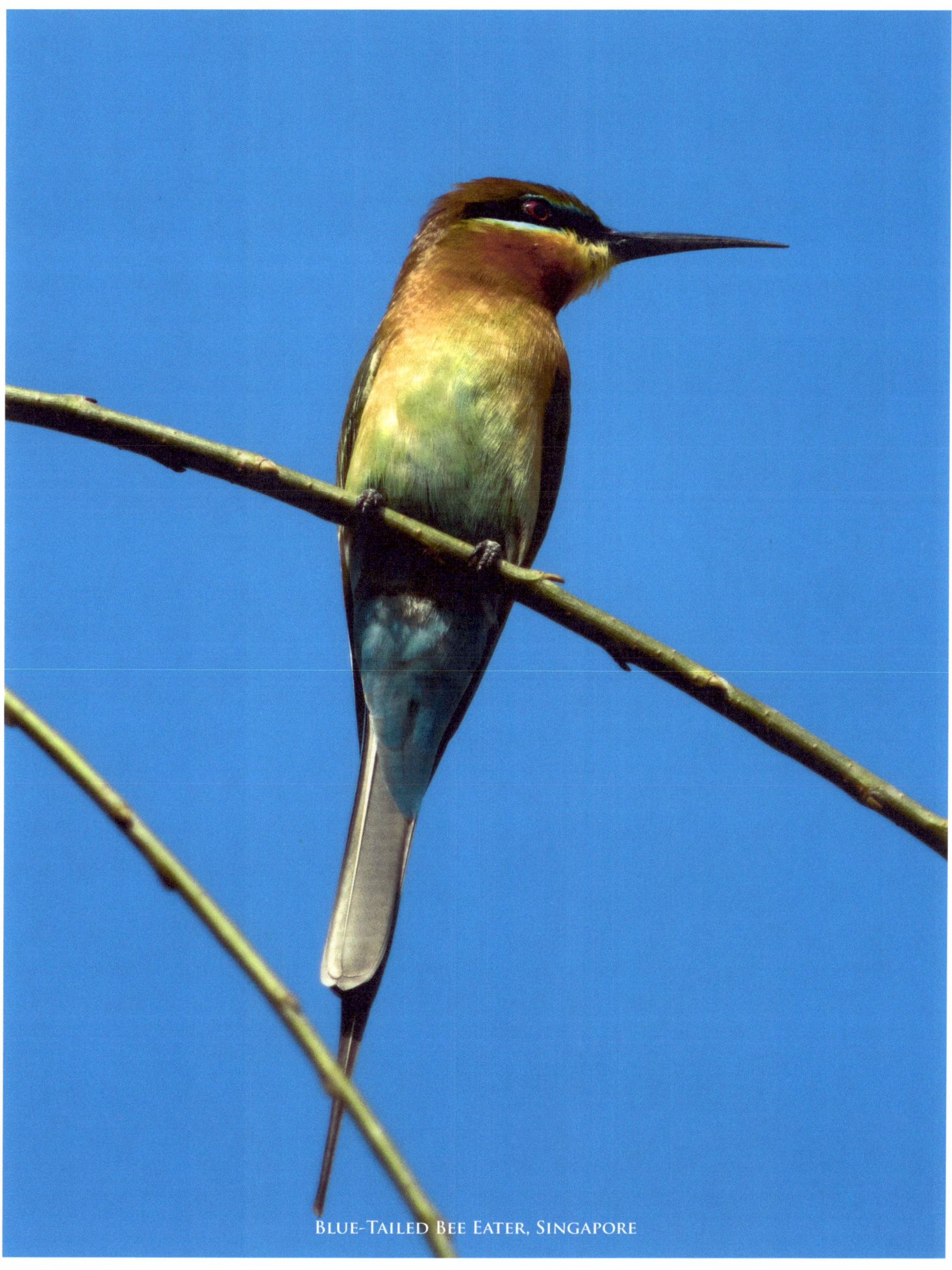

Blue-Tailed Bee Eater, Singapore

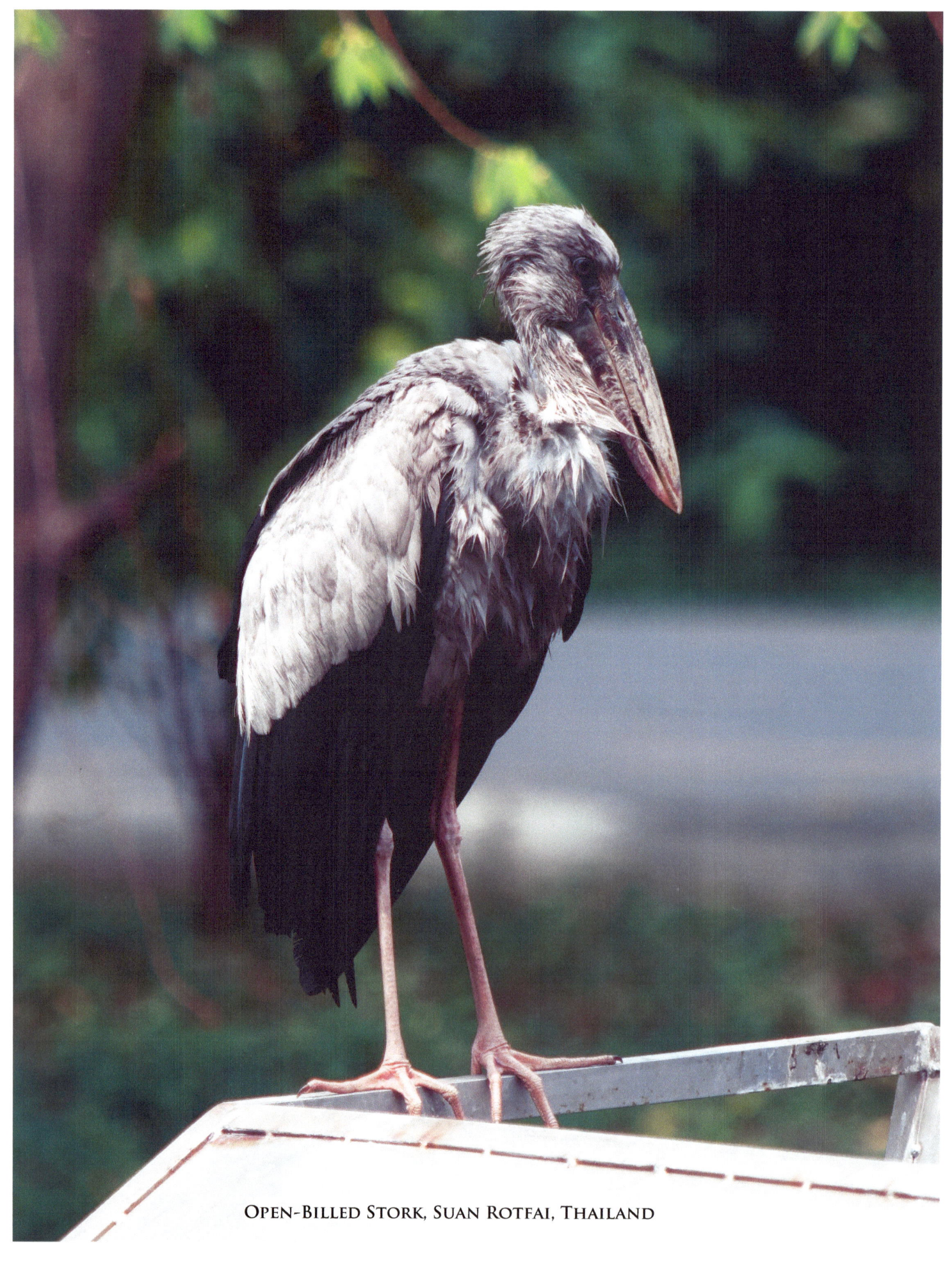

Open-Billed Stork, Suan Rotfai, Thailand

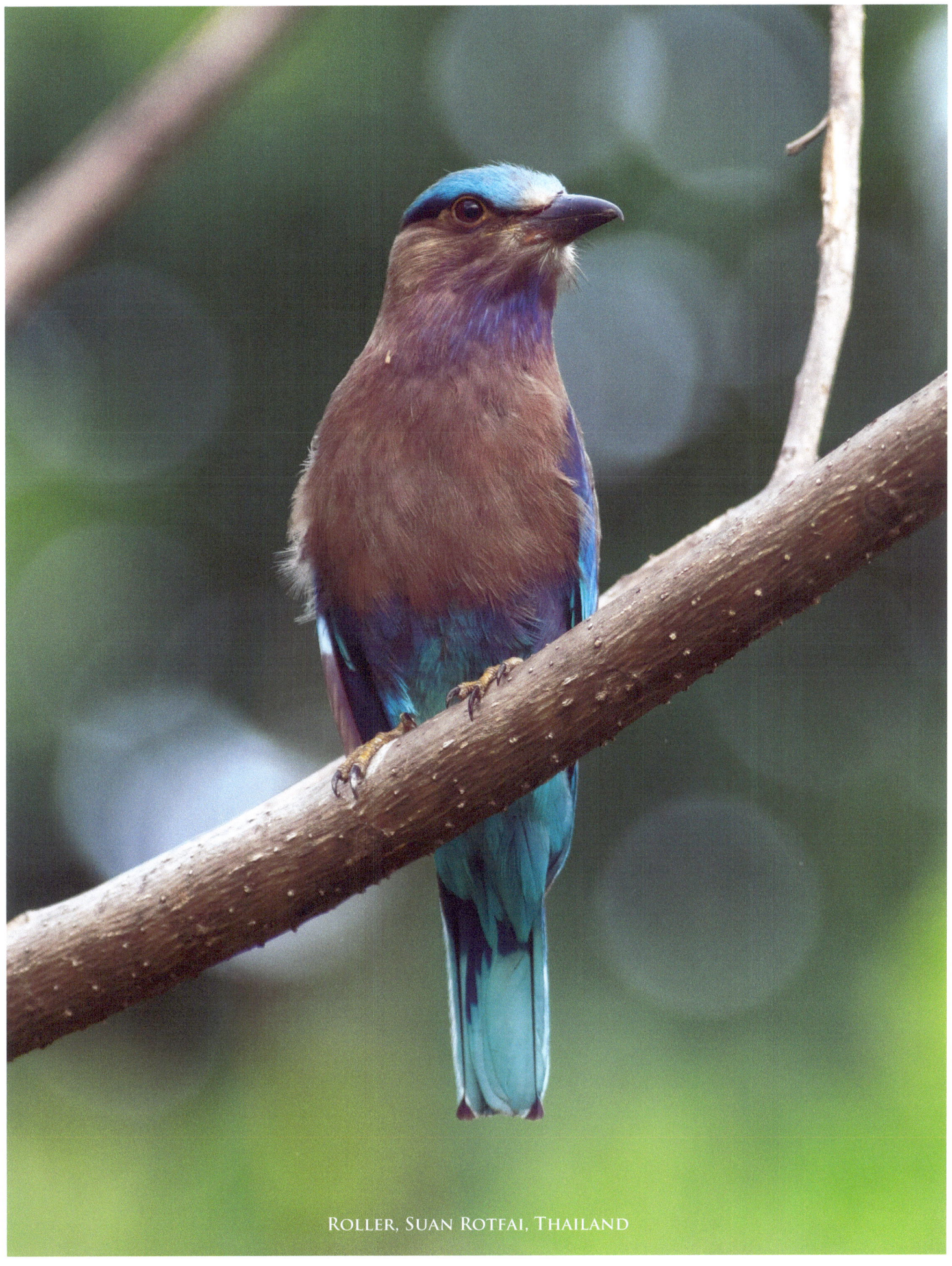

Roller, Suan Rotfai, Thailand

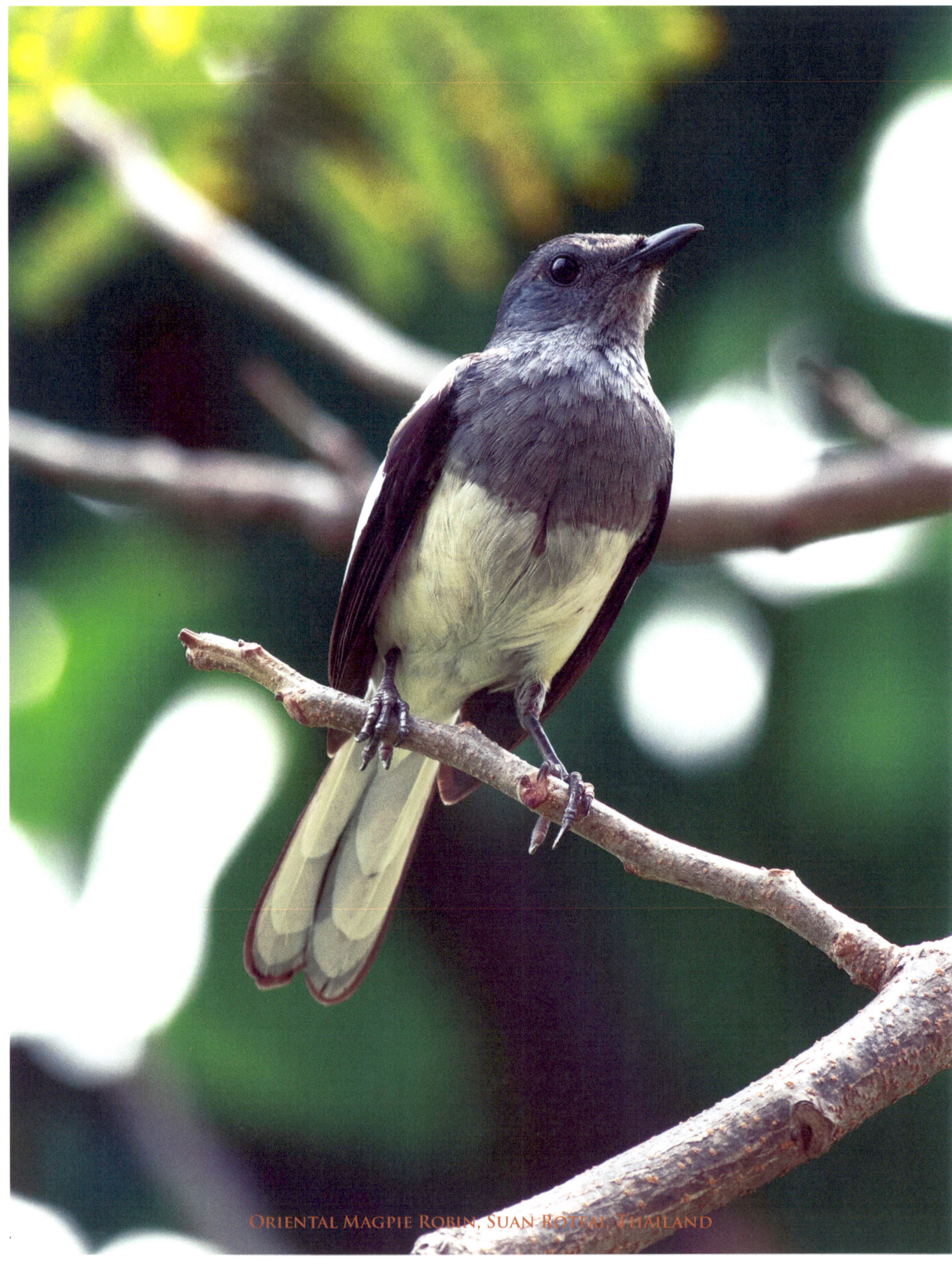

ORIENTAL MAGPIE ROBIN, SUAN ROTFAI, THAILAND

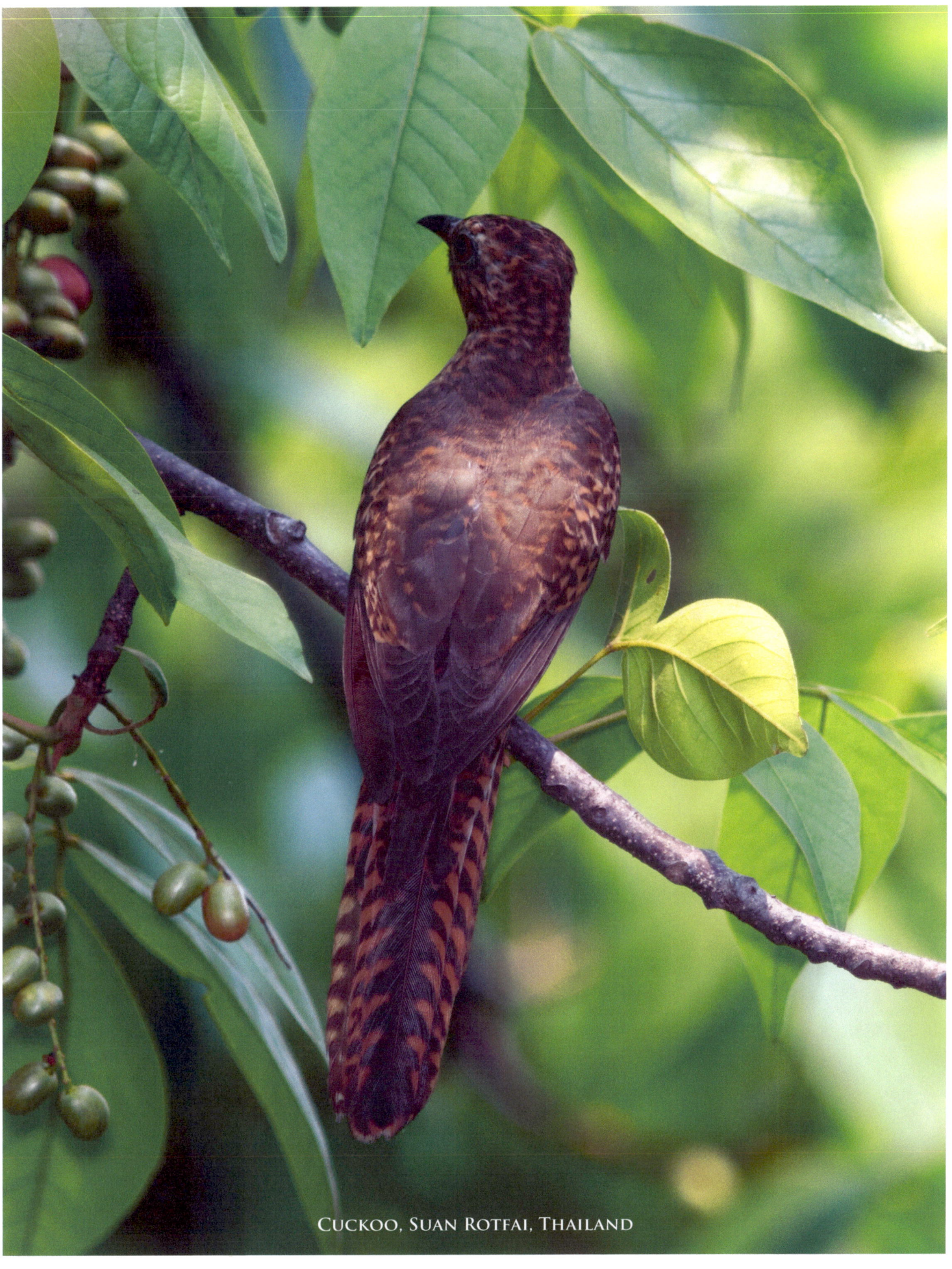

CUCKOO, SUAN ROTFAI, THAILAND

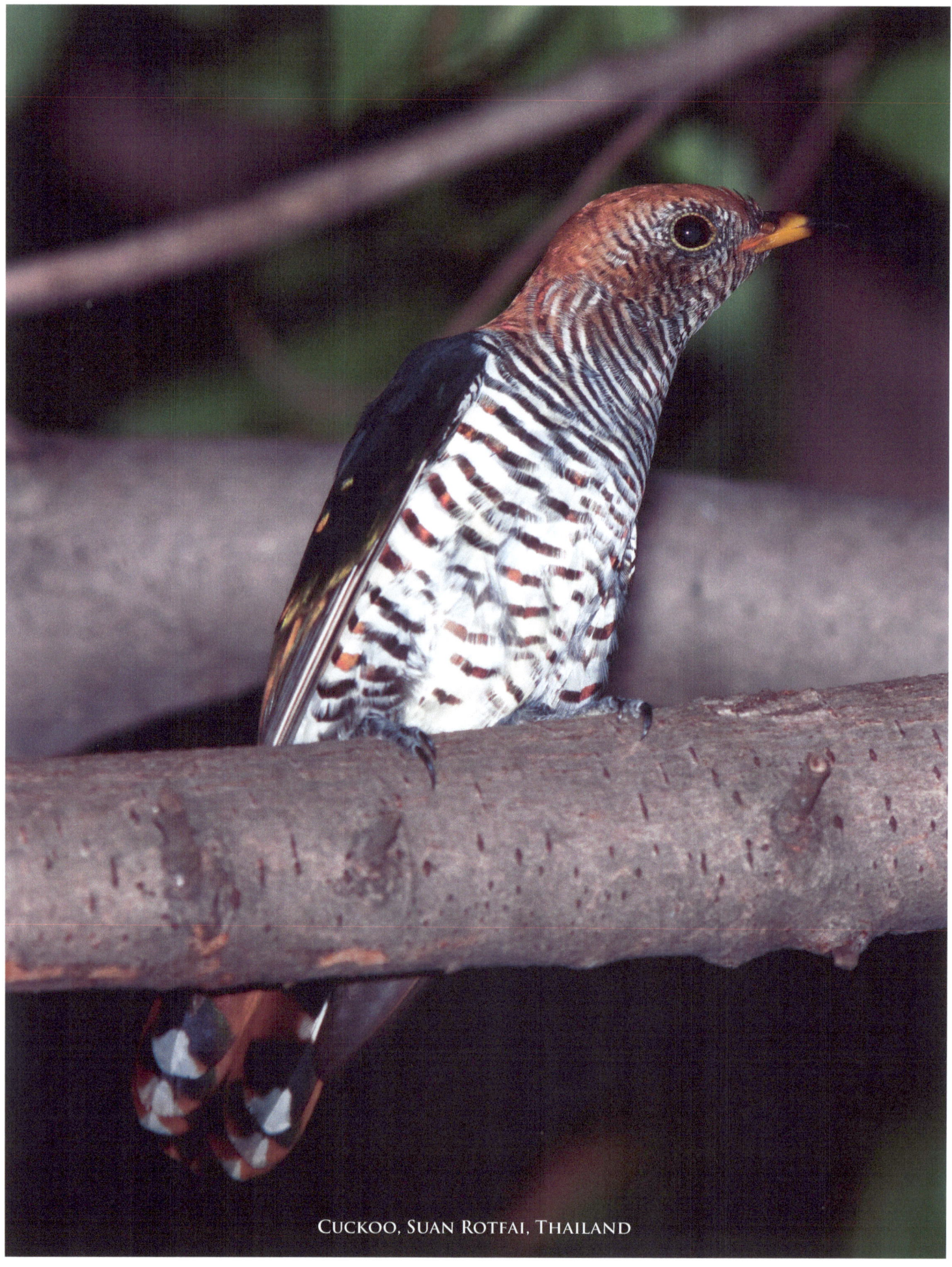

CUCKOO, SUAN ROTFAI, THAILAND

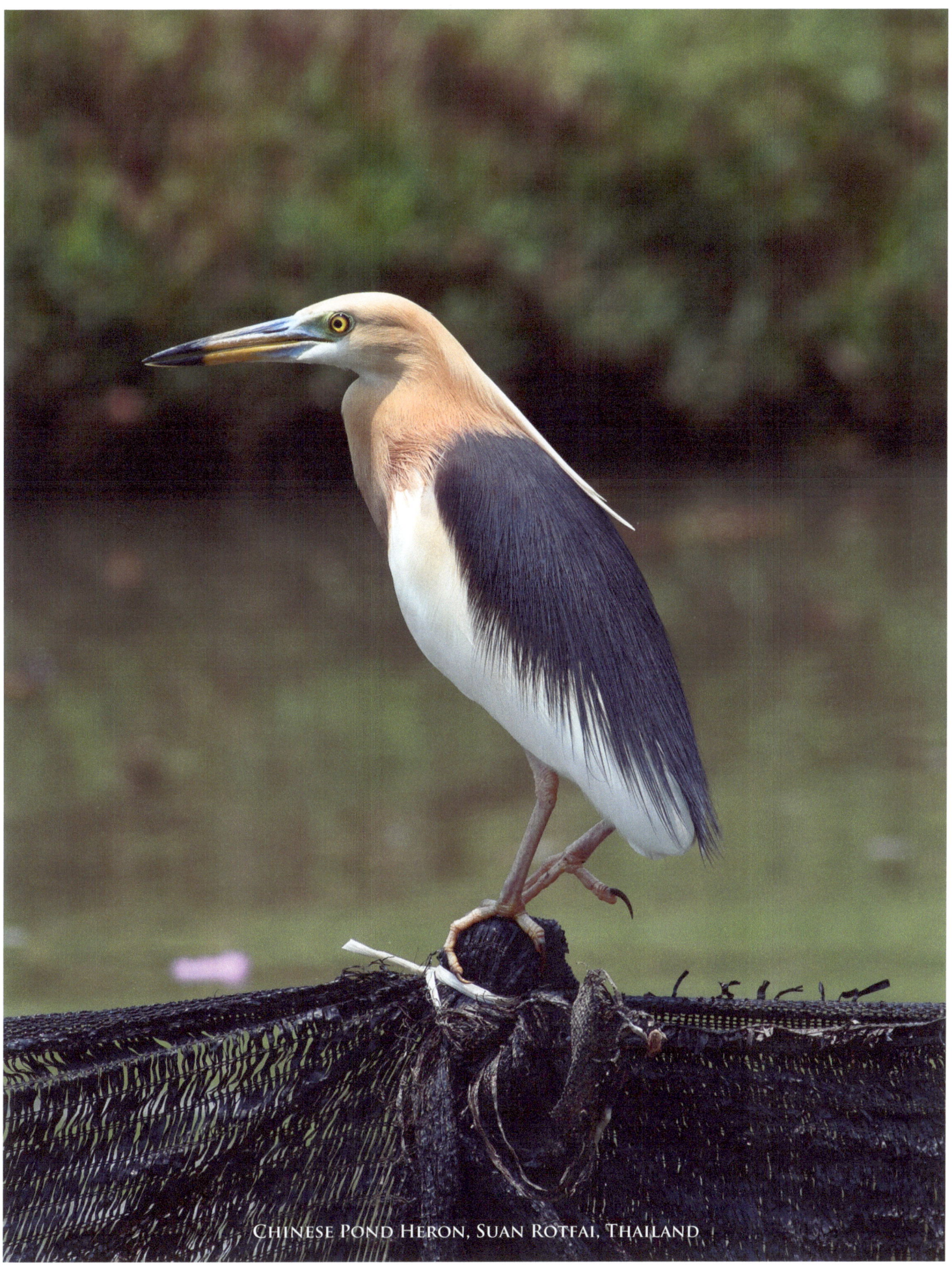

CHINESE POND HERON, SUAN ROTFAI, THAILAND

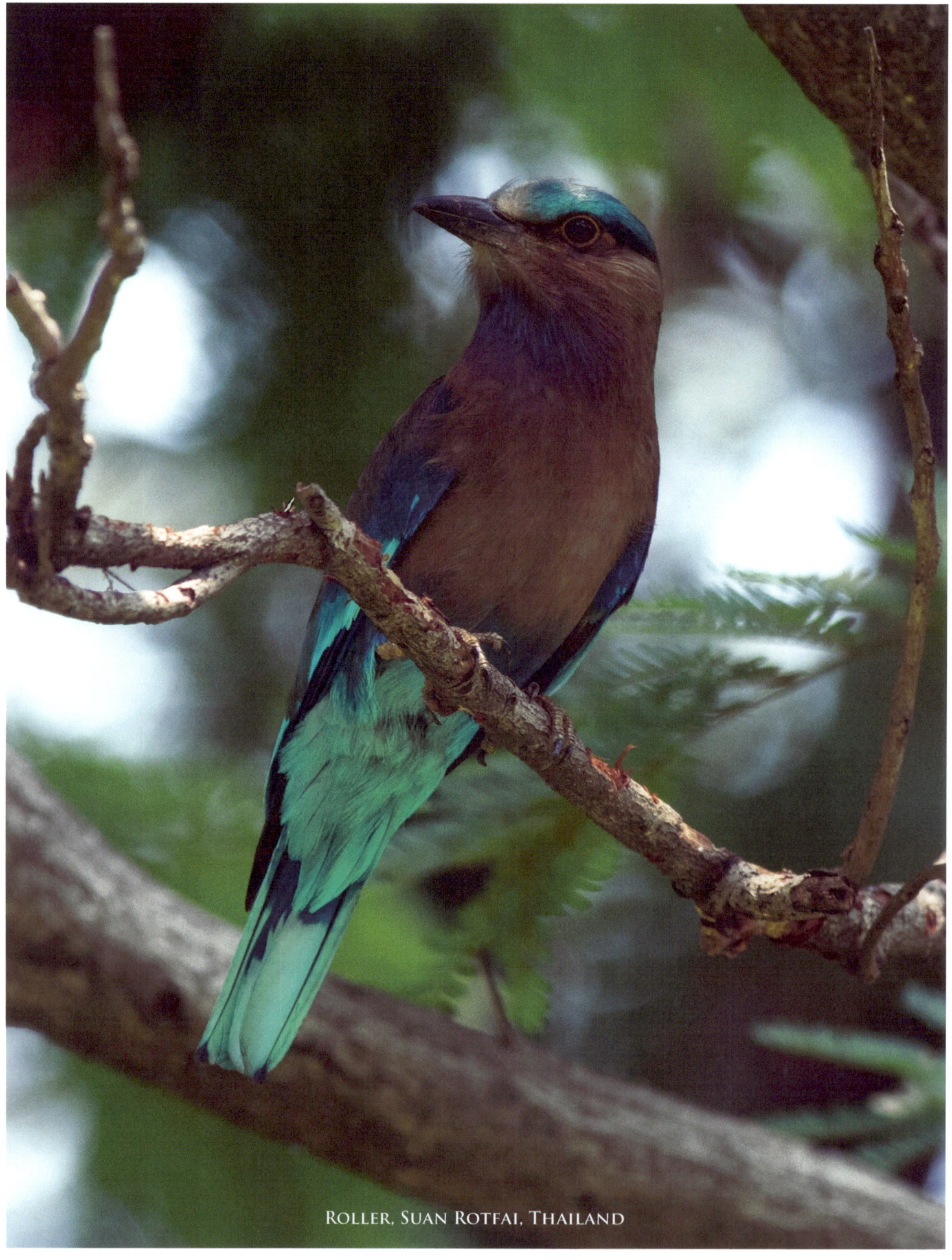

ROLLER, SUAN ROTFAI, THAILAND

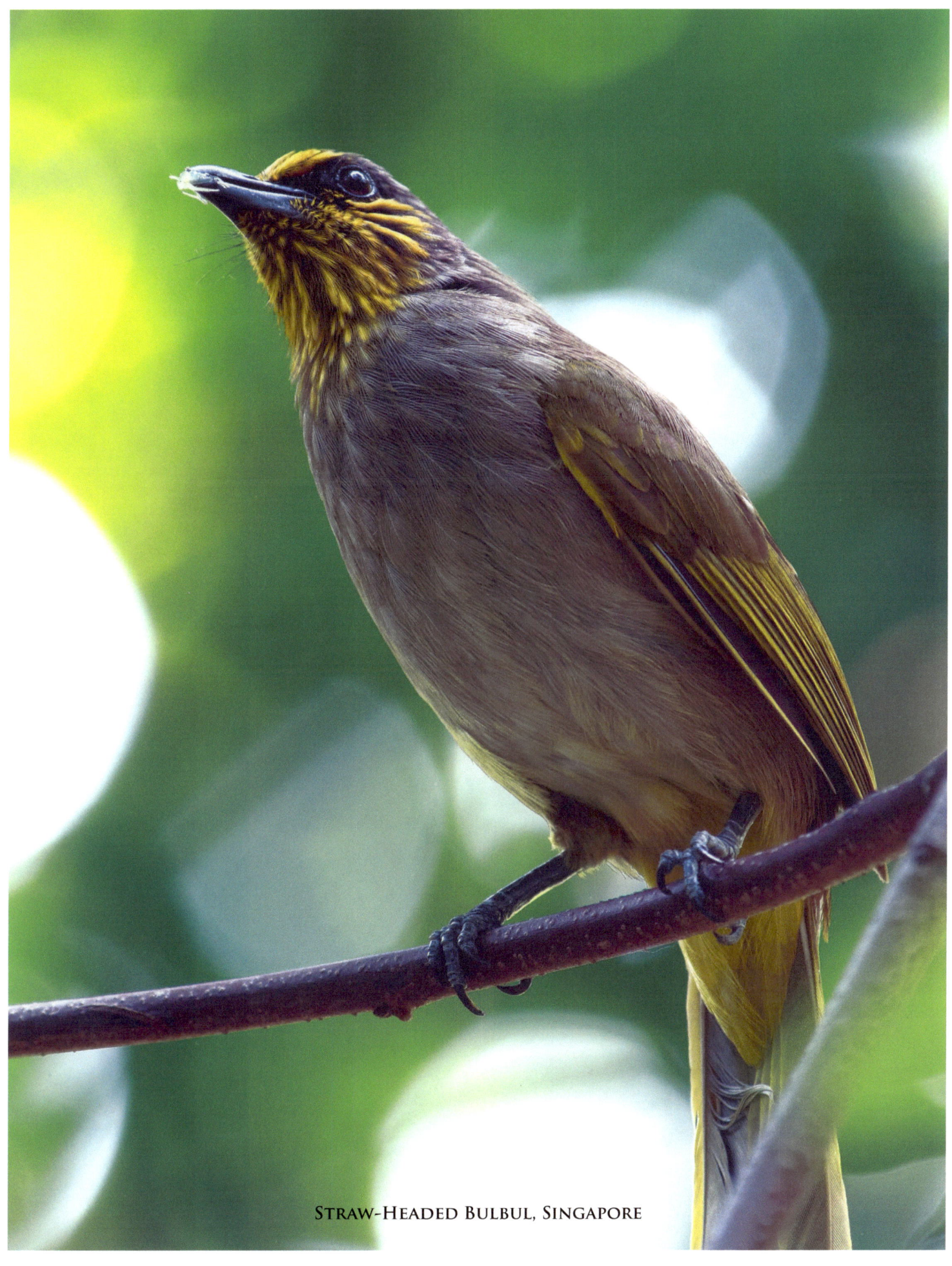

STRAW-HEADED BULBUL, SINGAPORE

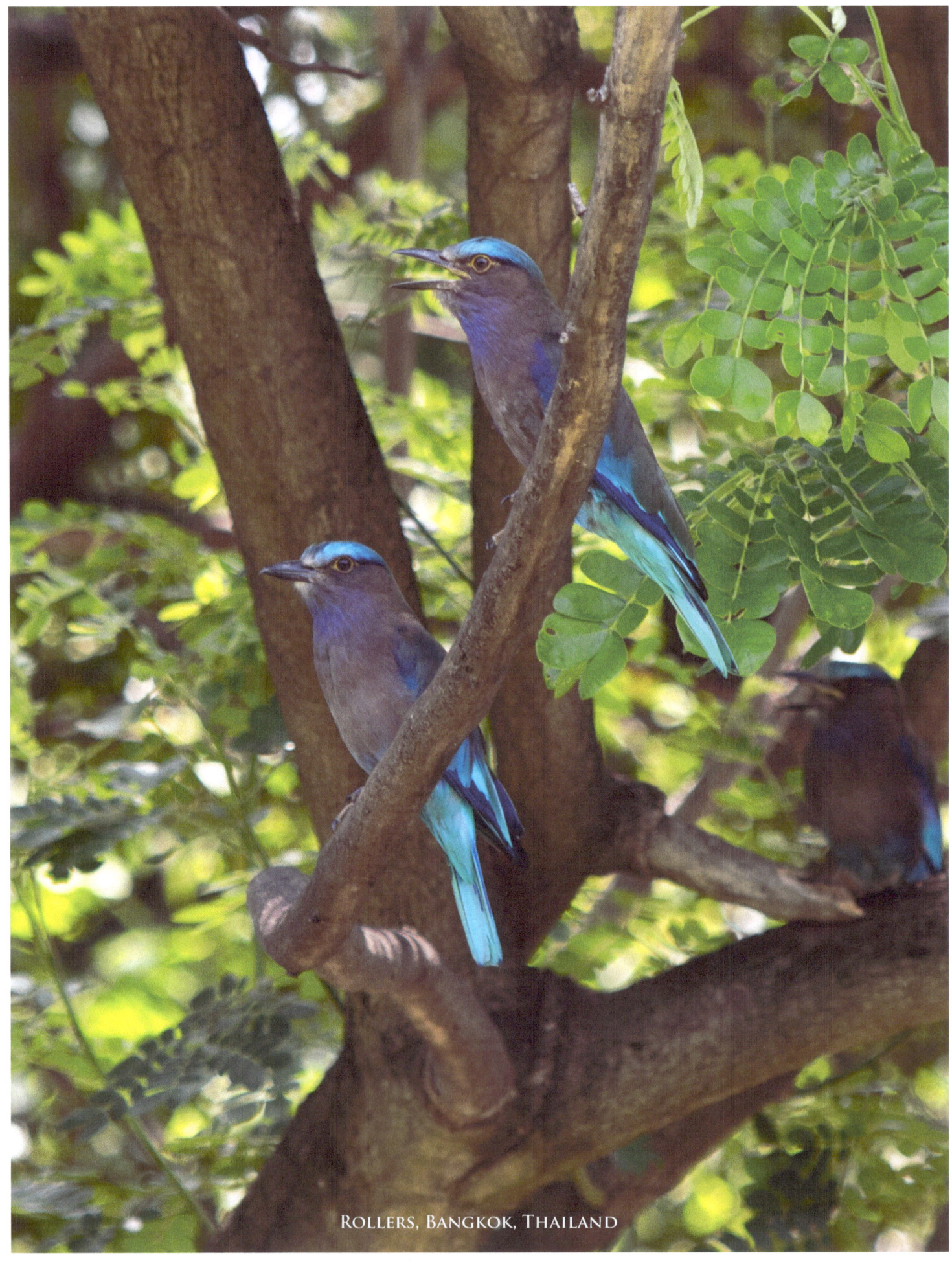

ROLLERS, BANGKOK, THAILAND

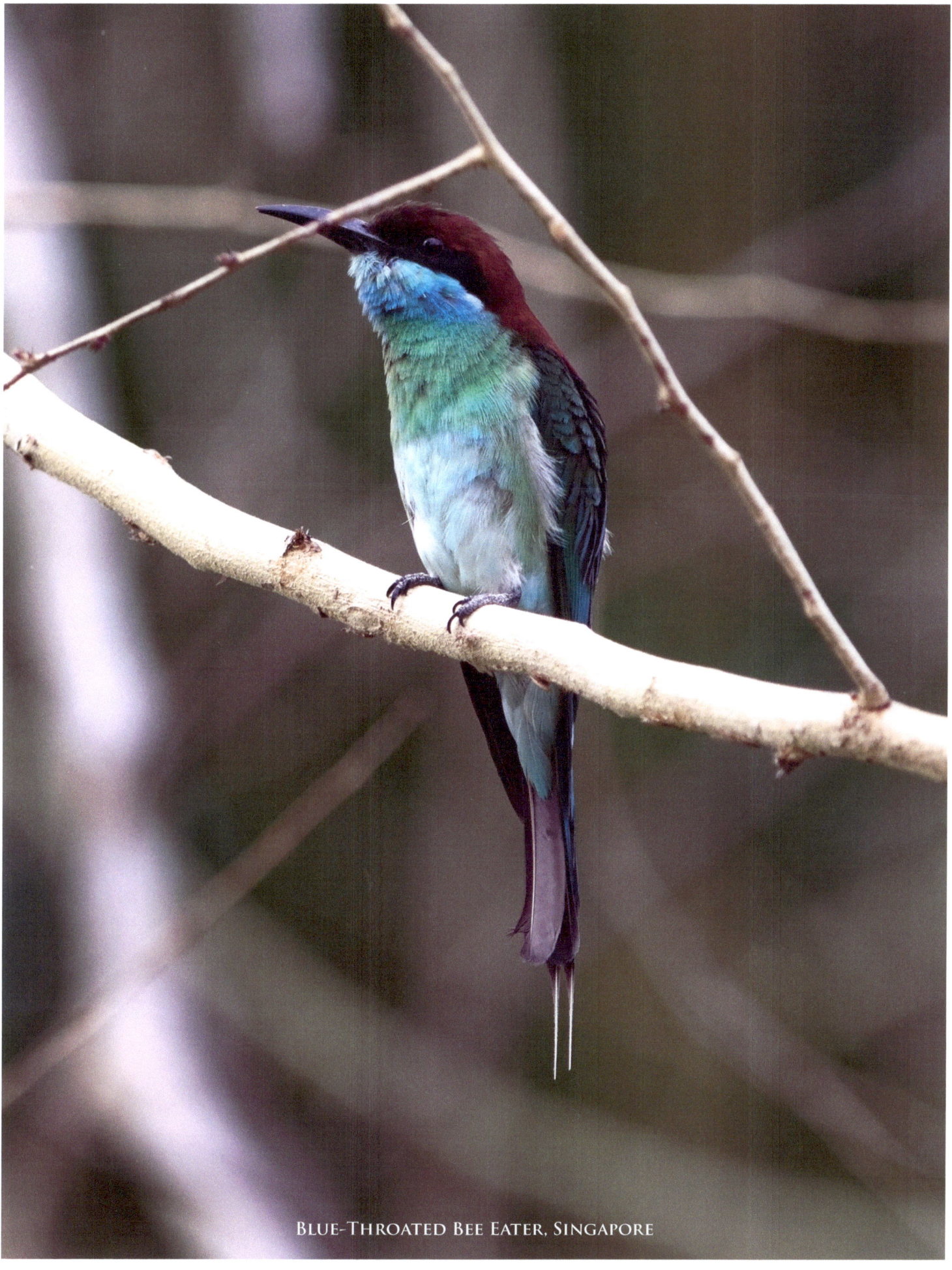

BLUE-THROATED BEE EATER, SINGAPORE

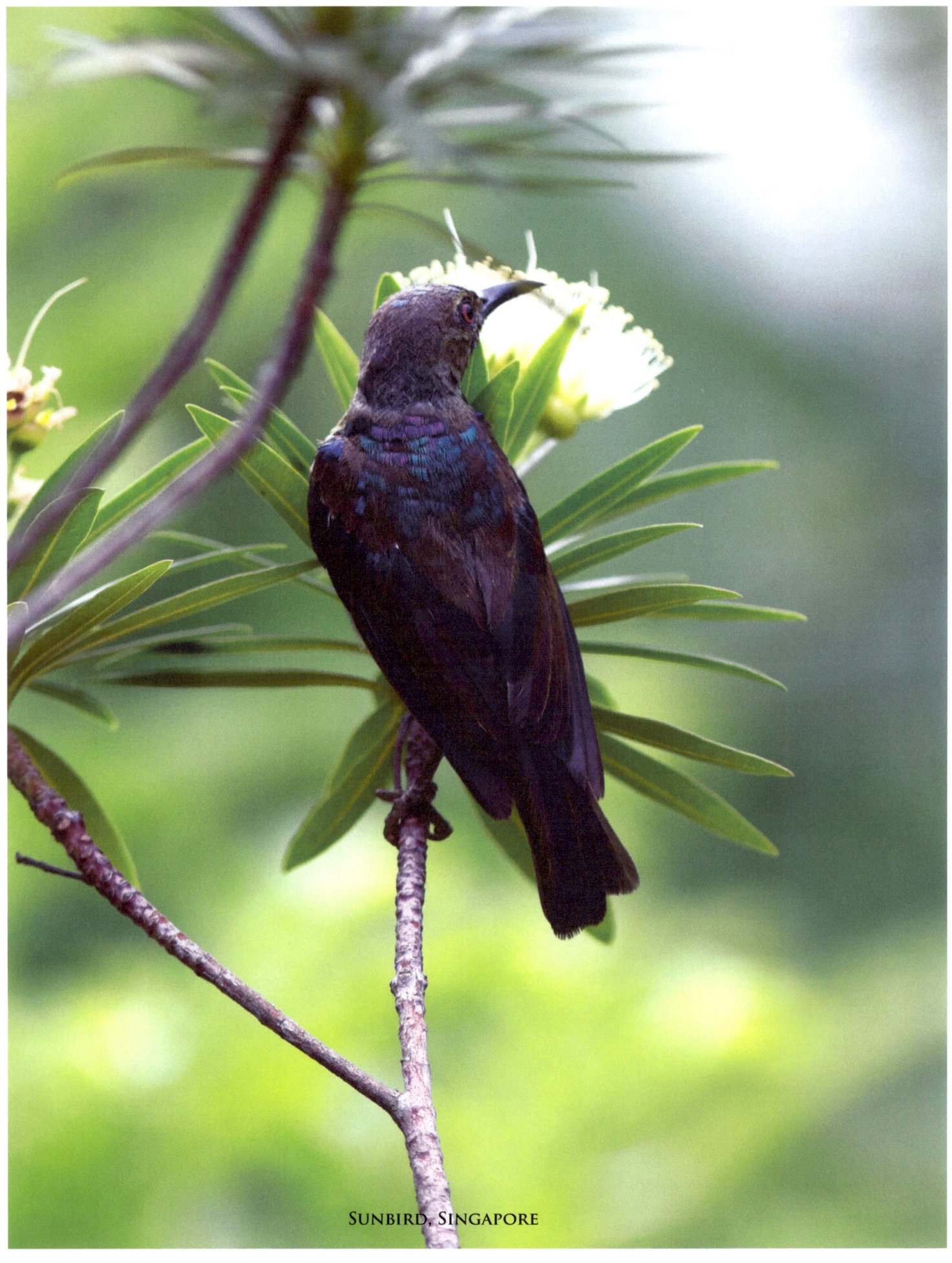

Sunbird, Singapore

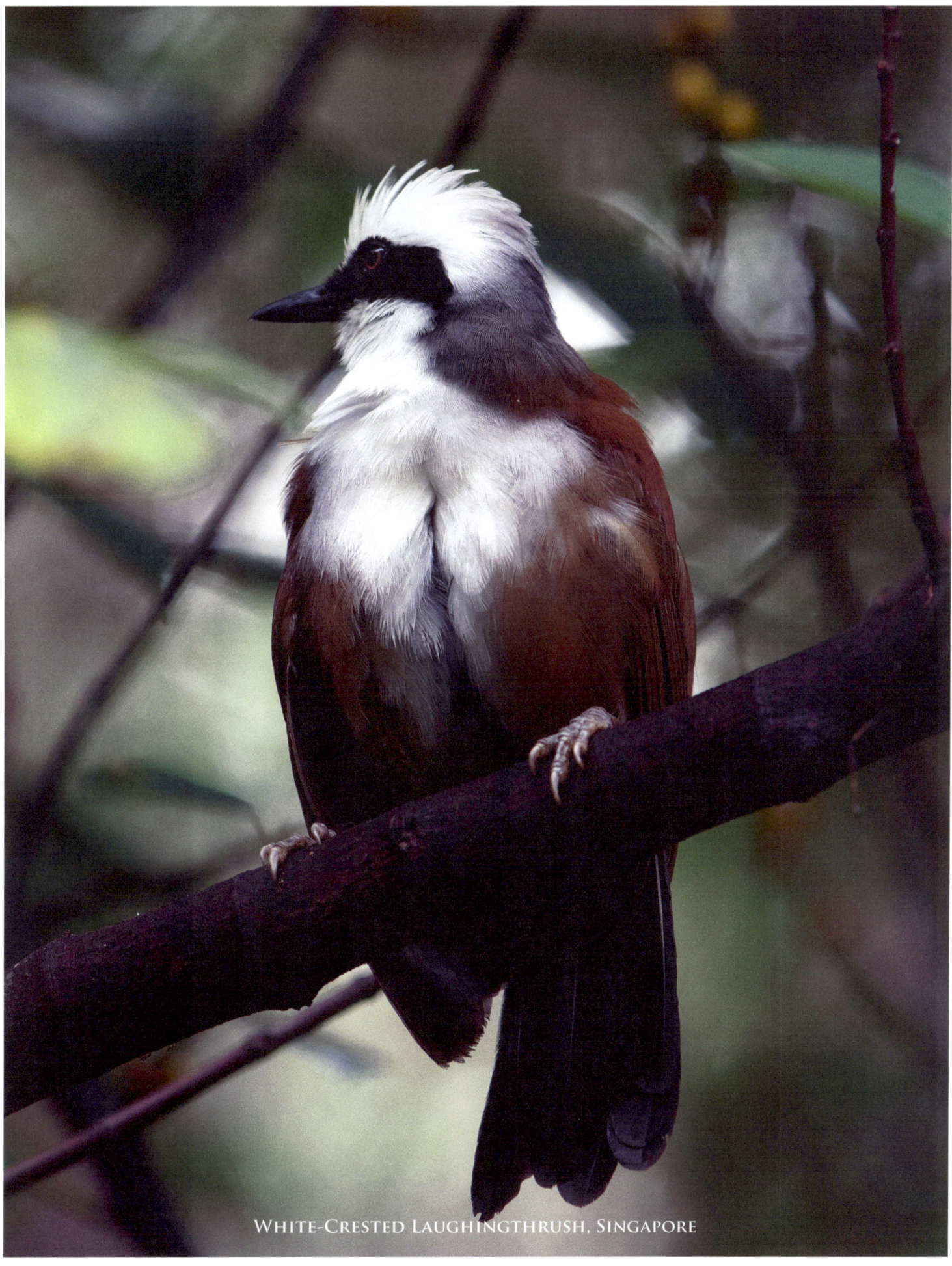

White-Crested Laughingthrush, Singapore

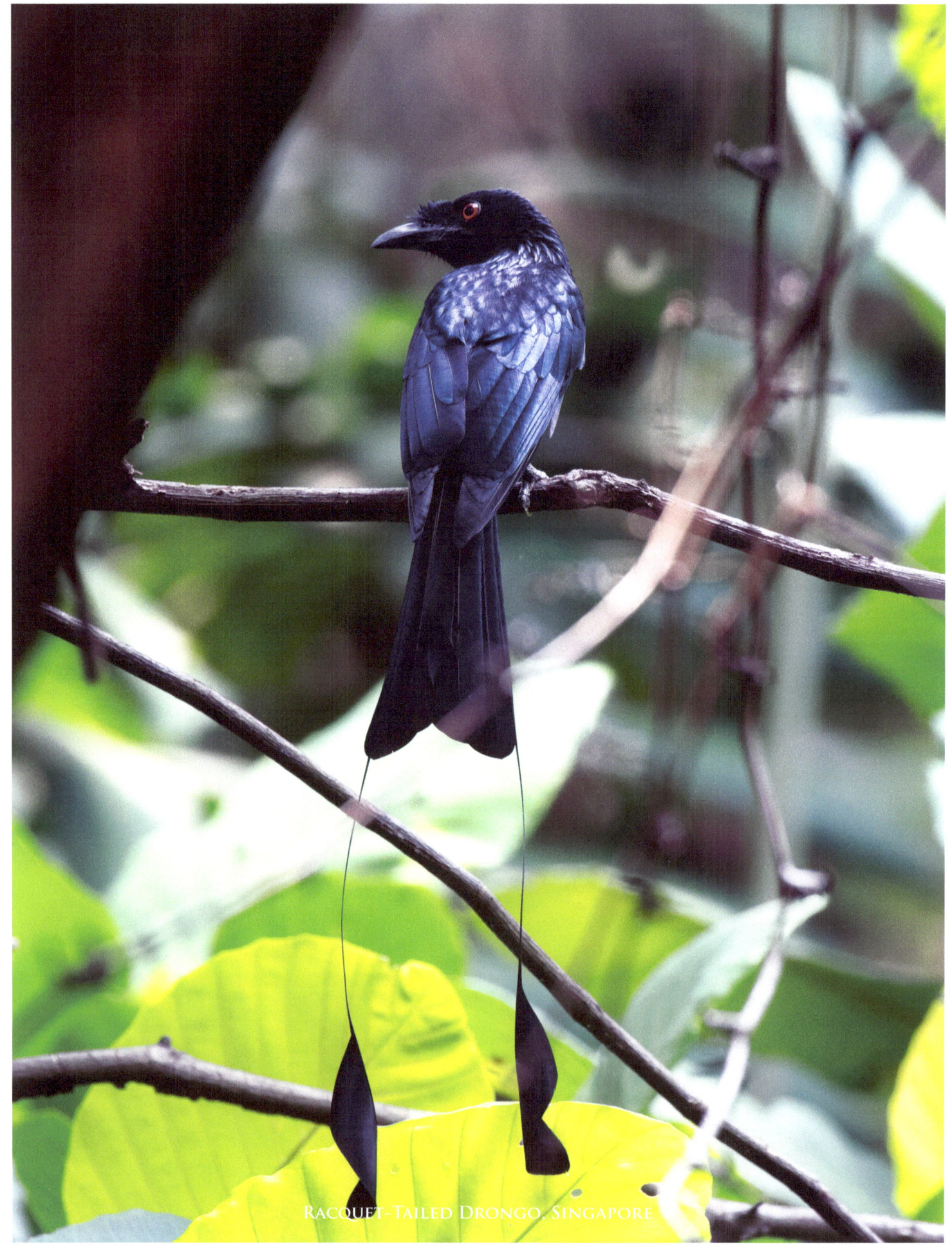

RACQUET-TAILED DRONGO, SINGAPORE

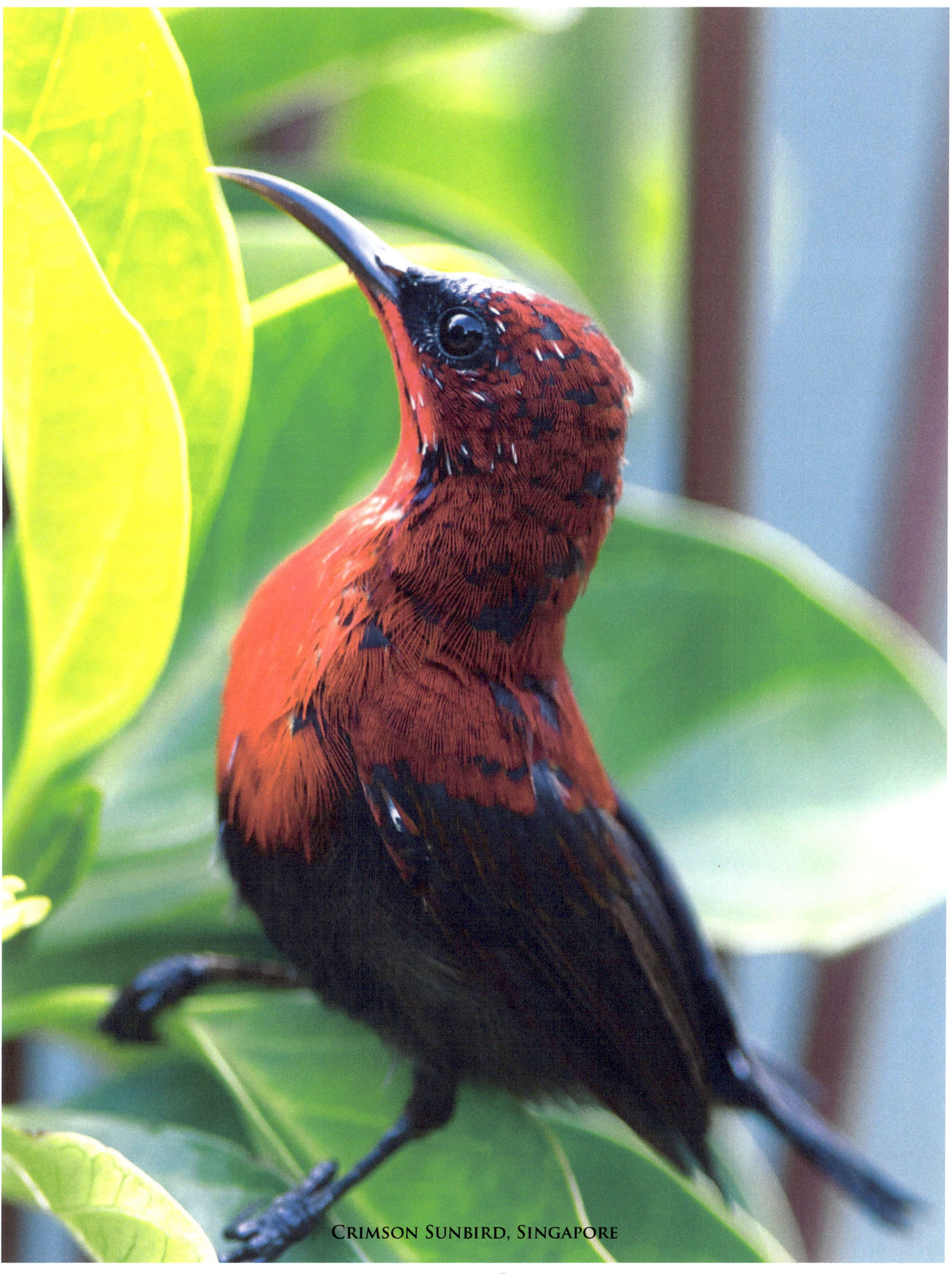

CRIMSON SUNBIRD, SINGAPORE

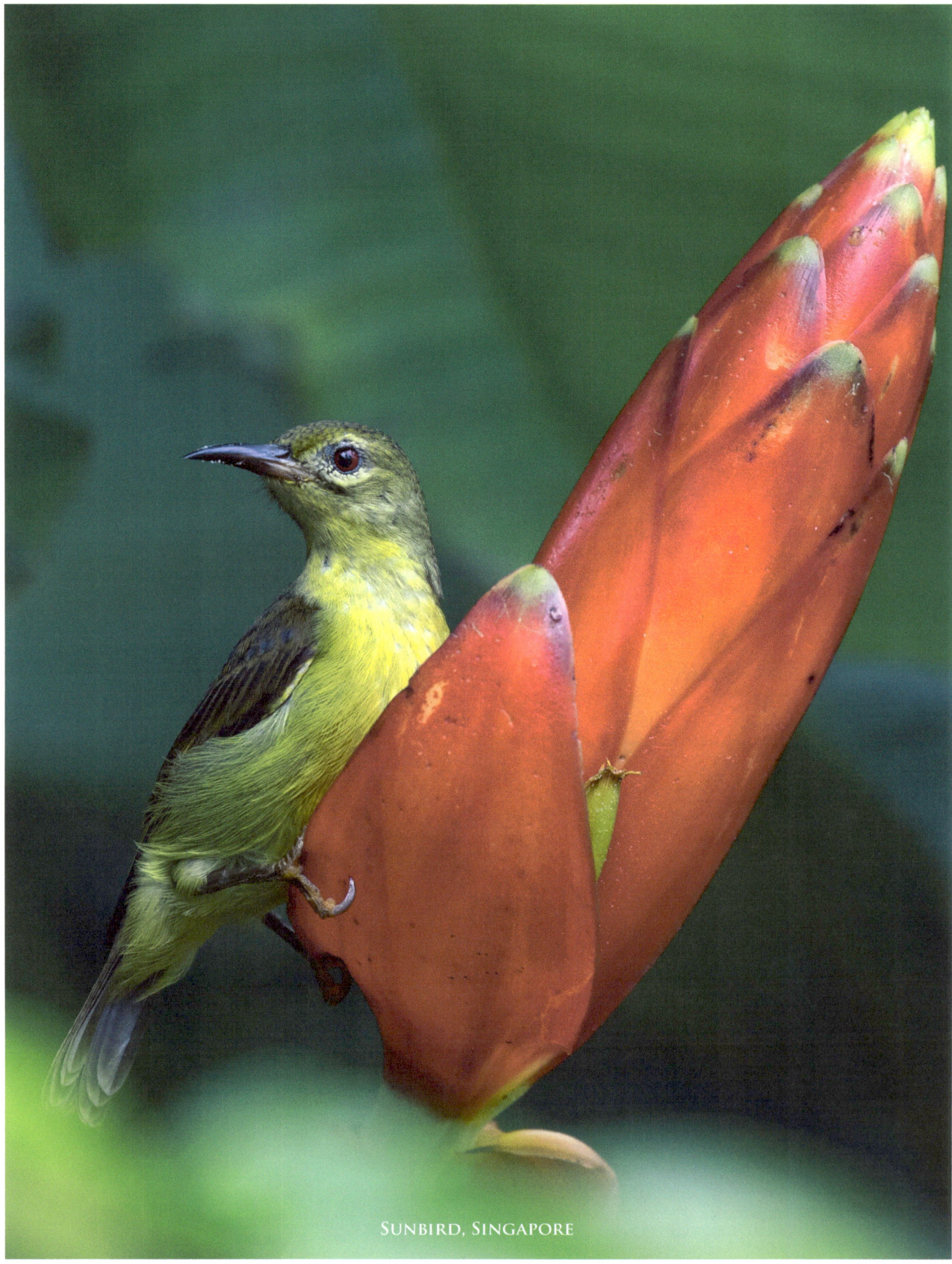

SUNBIRD, SINGAPORE

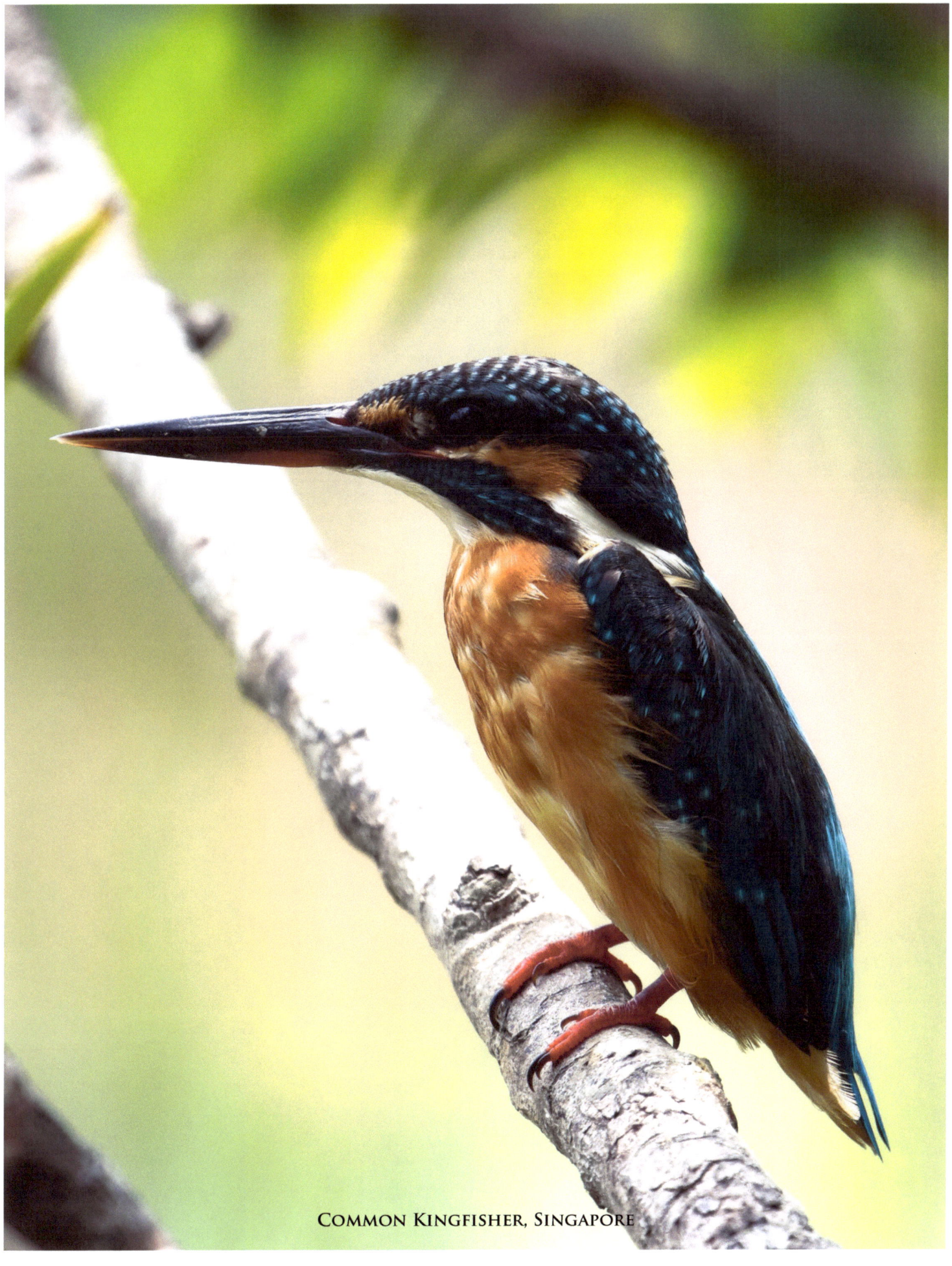

COMMON KINGFISHER, SINGAPORE

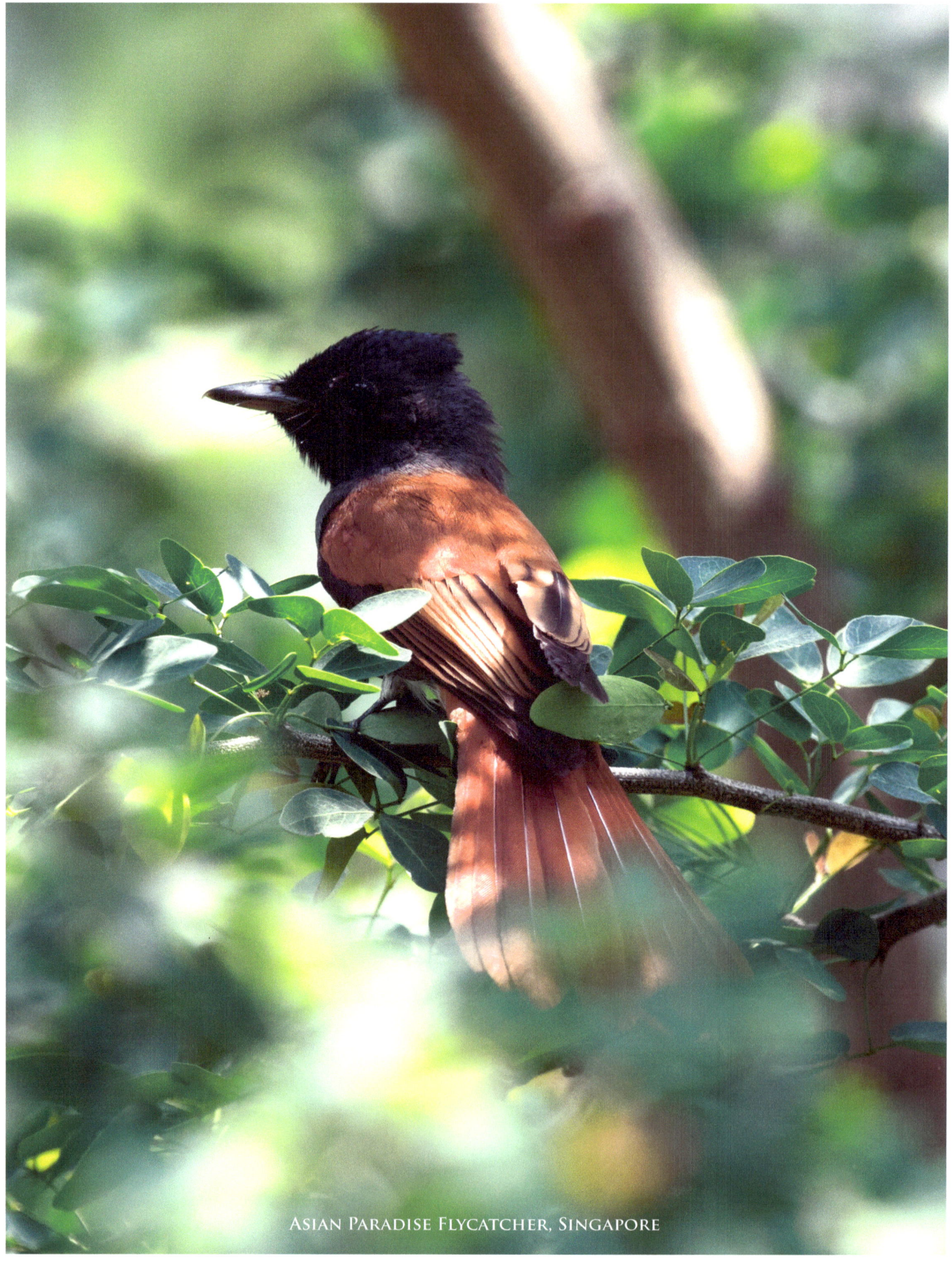

Asian Paradise Flycatcher, Singapore

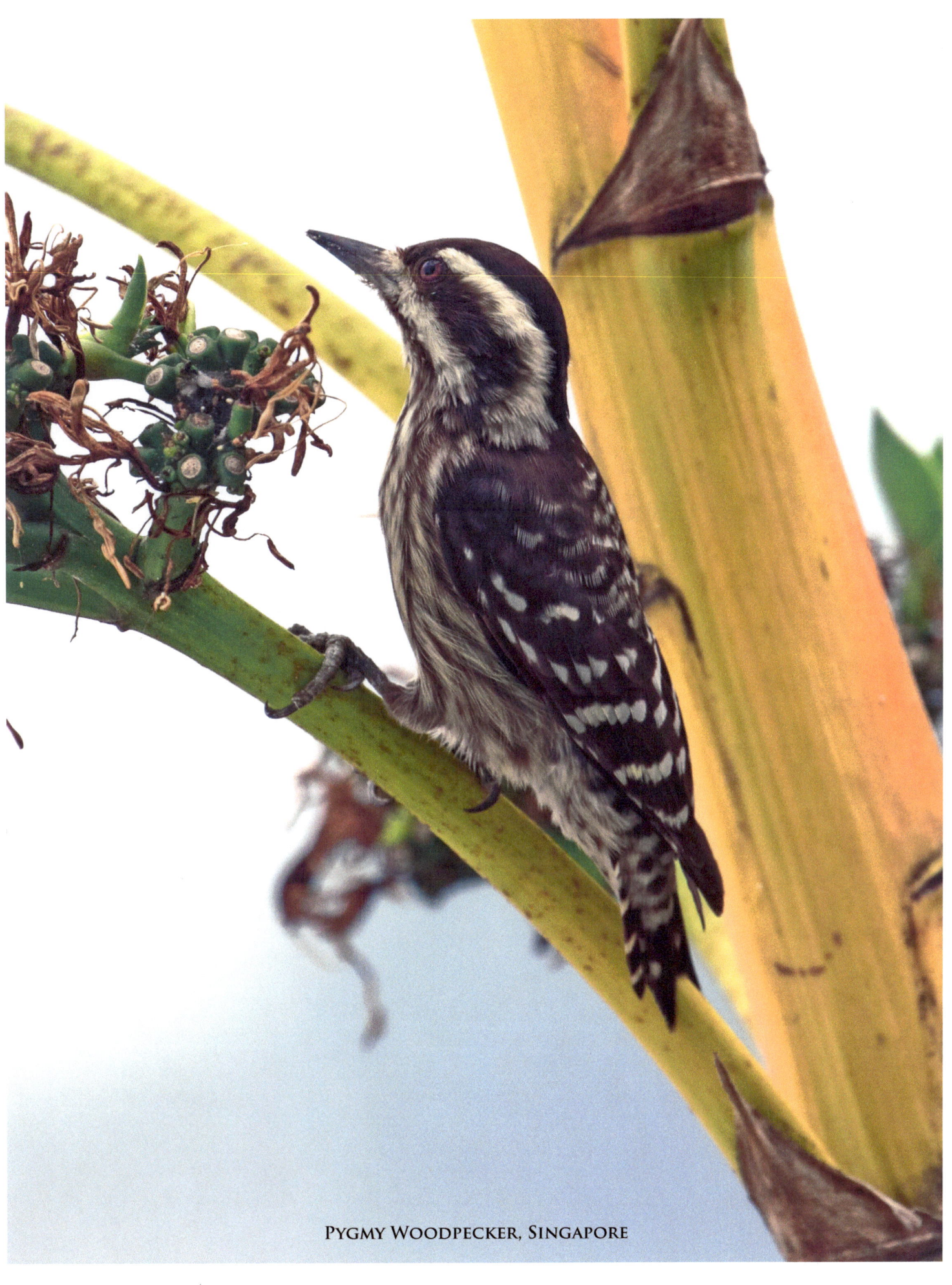

PYGMY WOODPECKER, SINGAPORE

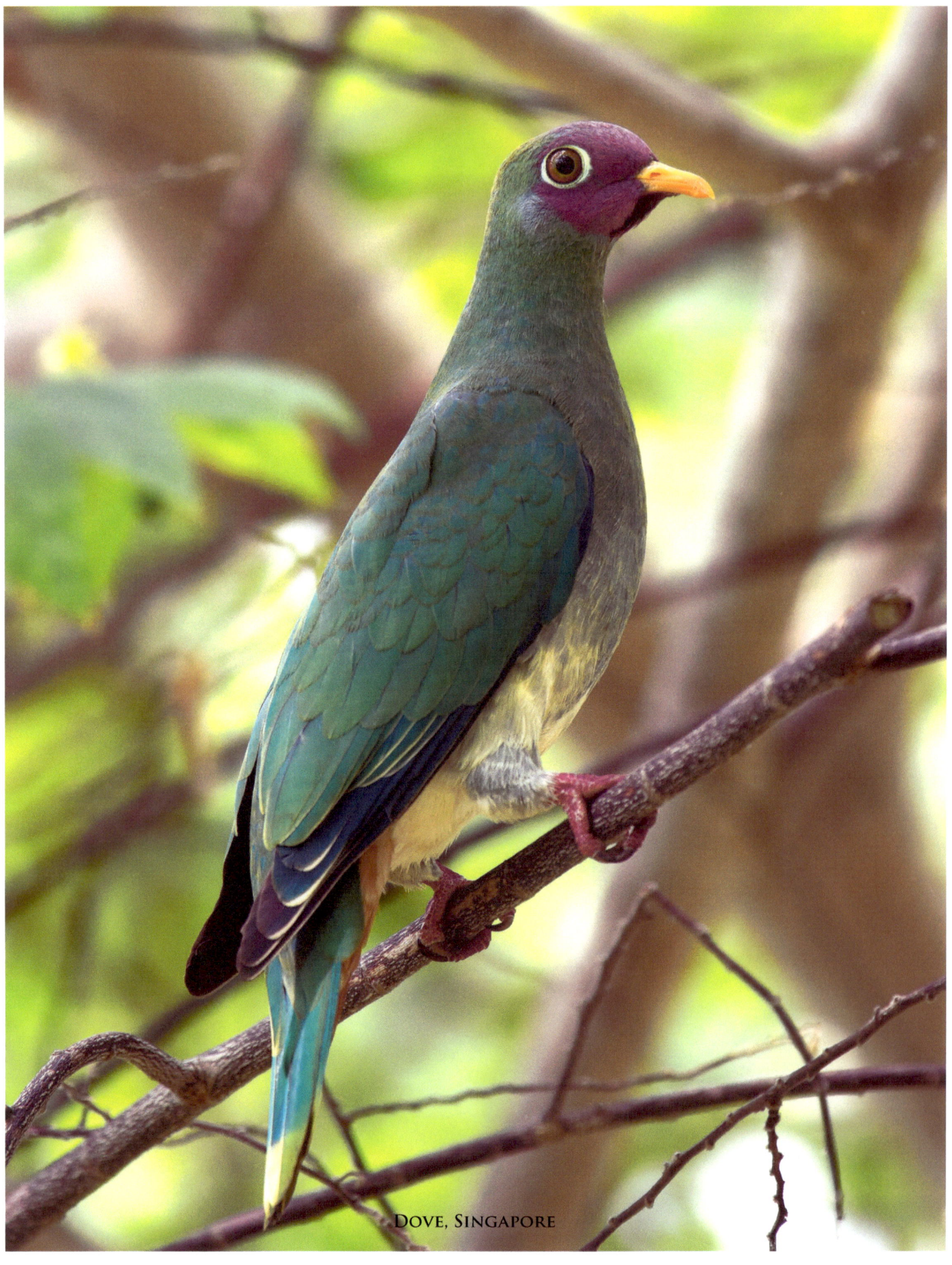

DOVE, SINGAPORE

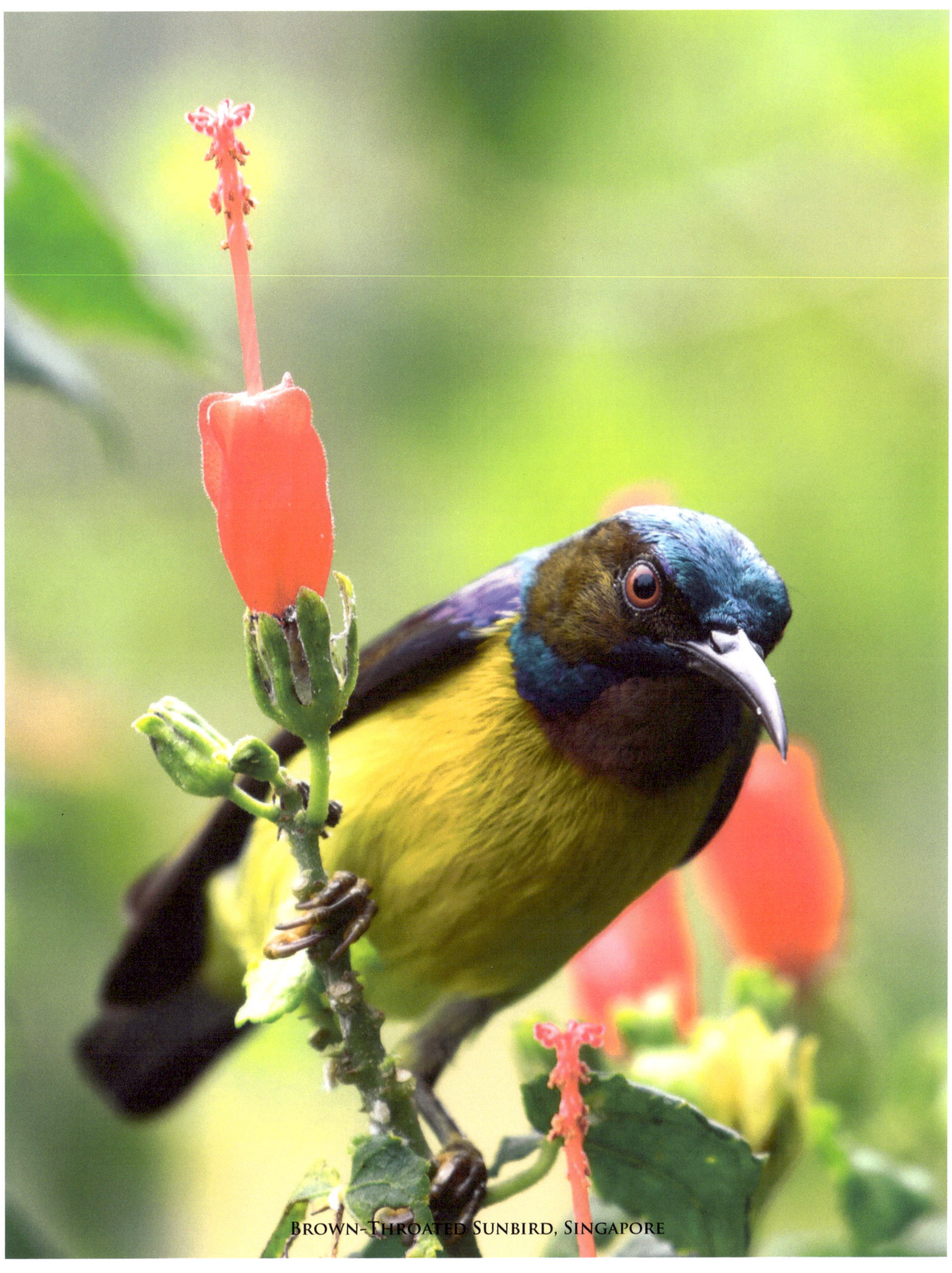

BROWN-THROATED SUNBIRD, SINGAPORE

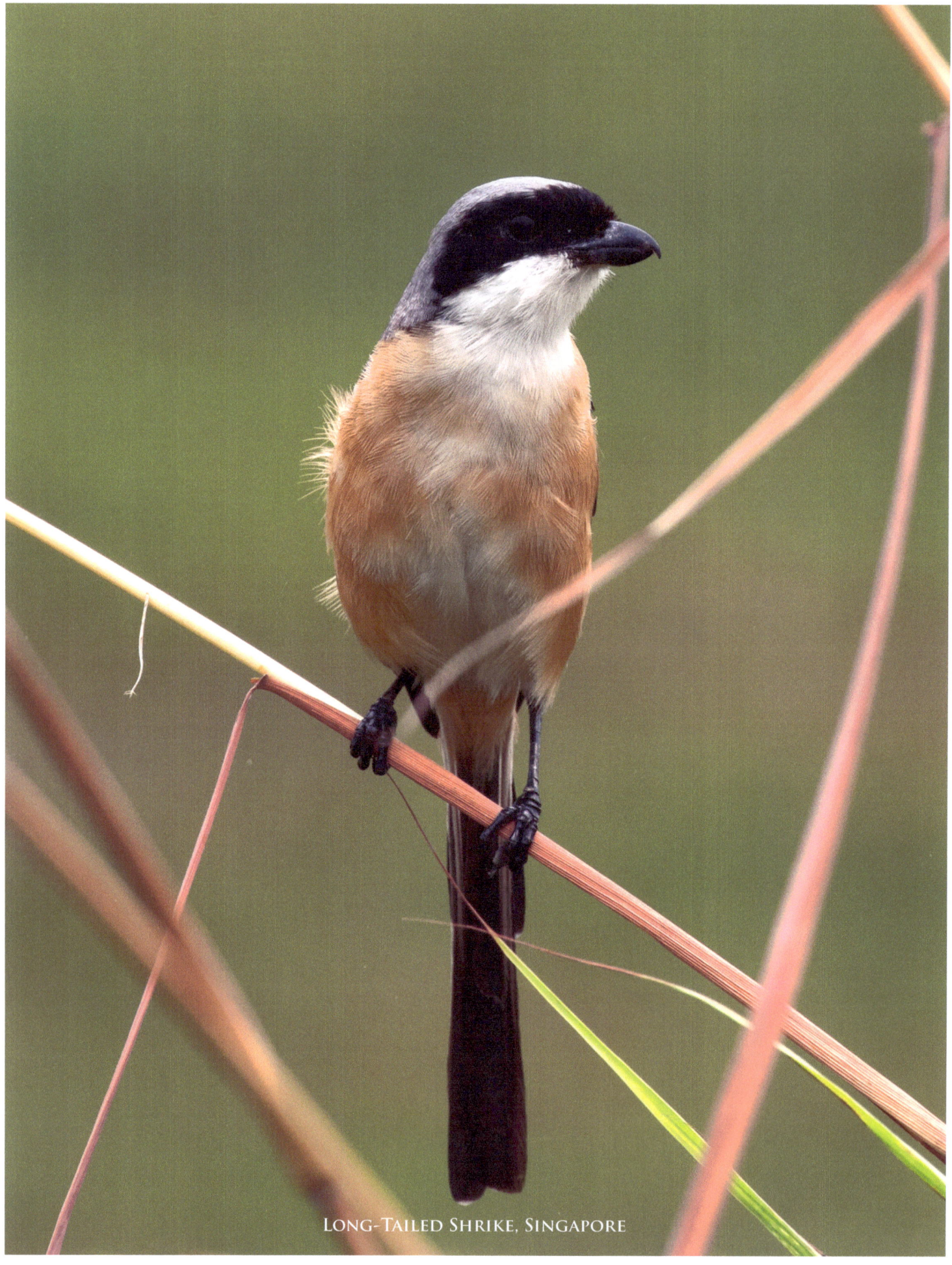

LONG-TAILED SHRIKE, SINGAPORE

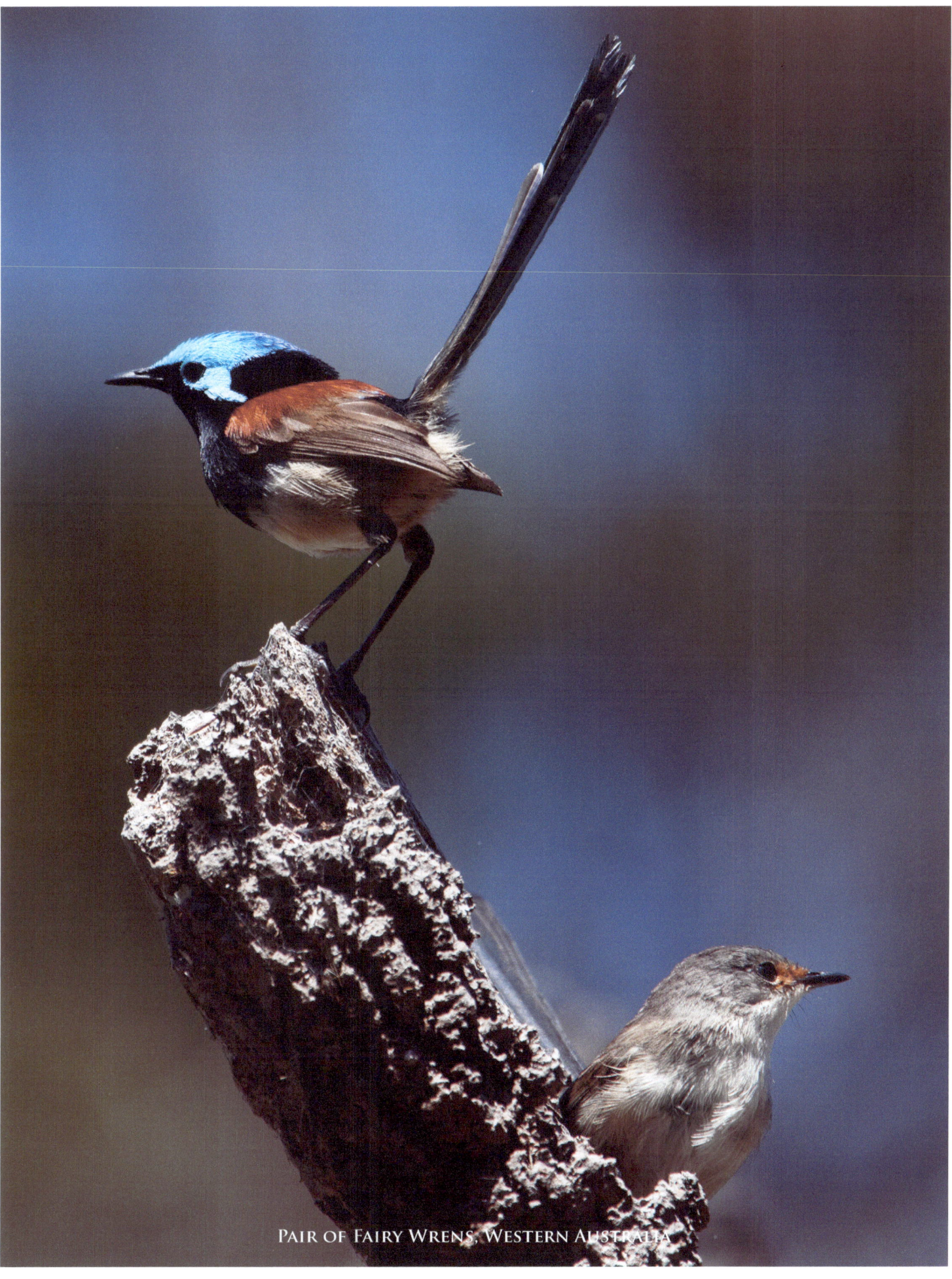

Pair of Fairy Wrens, Western Australia

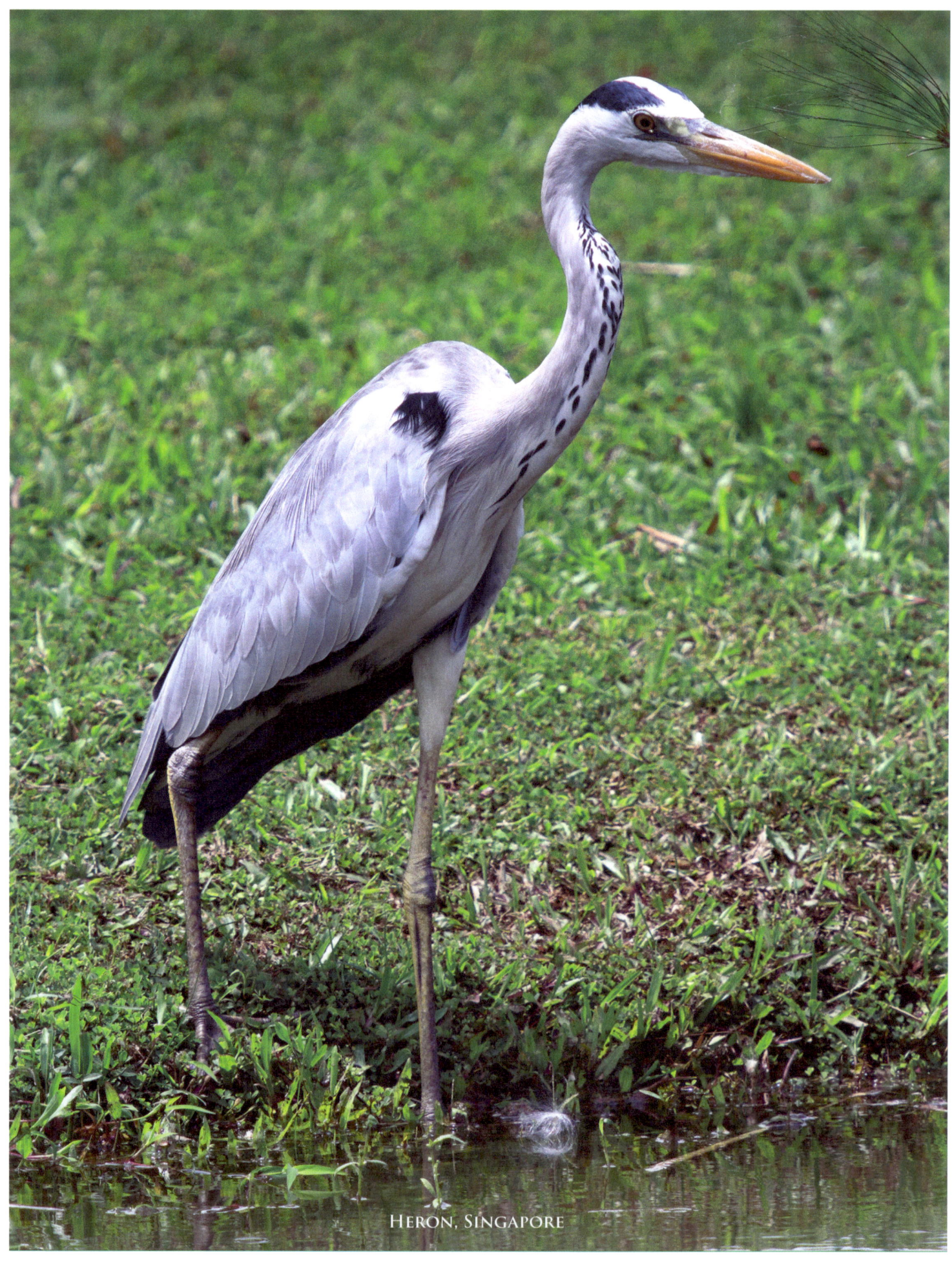

HERON, SINGAPORE

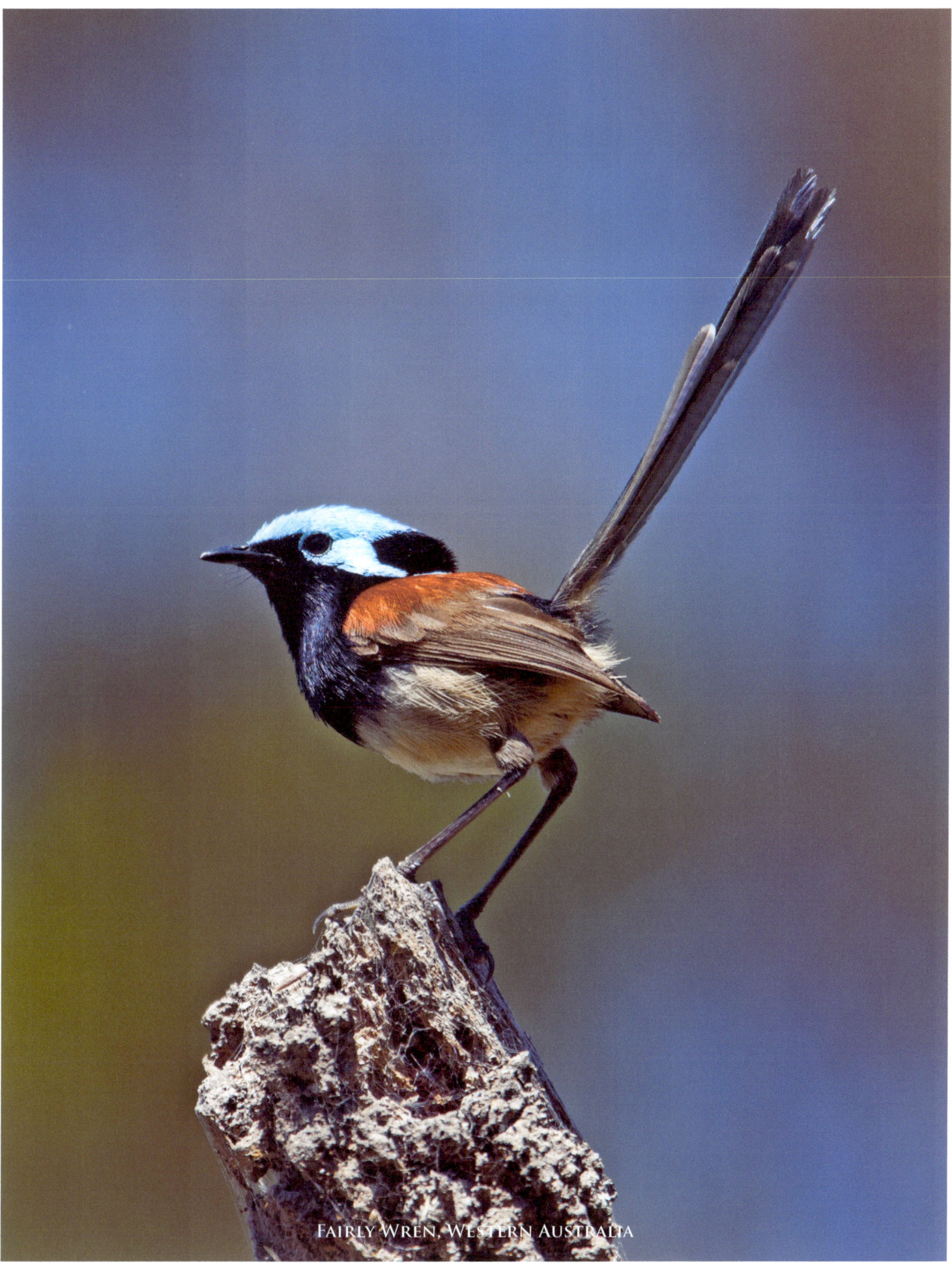

Fairly Wren, Western Australia

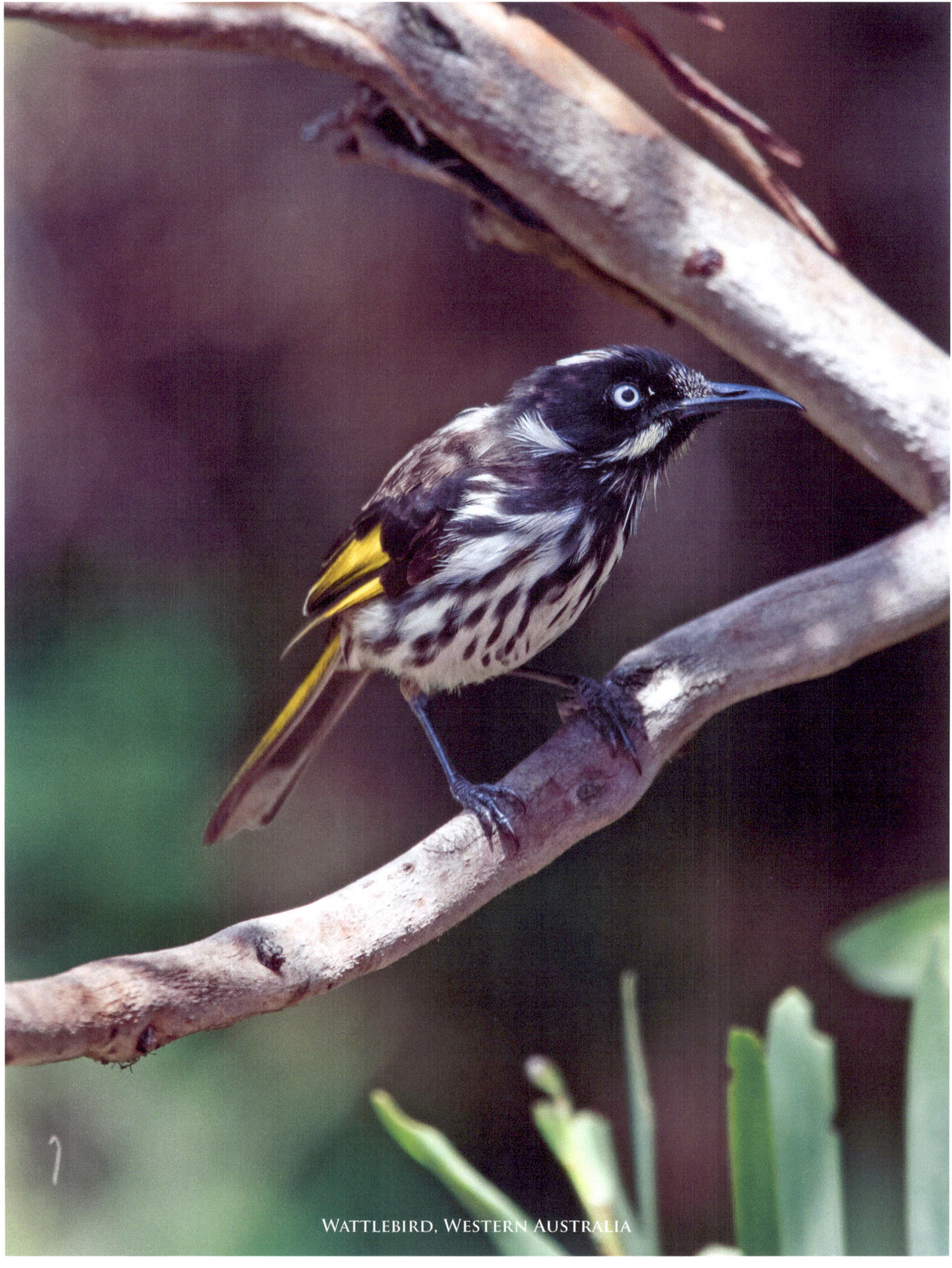

Wattlebird, Western Australia

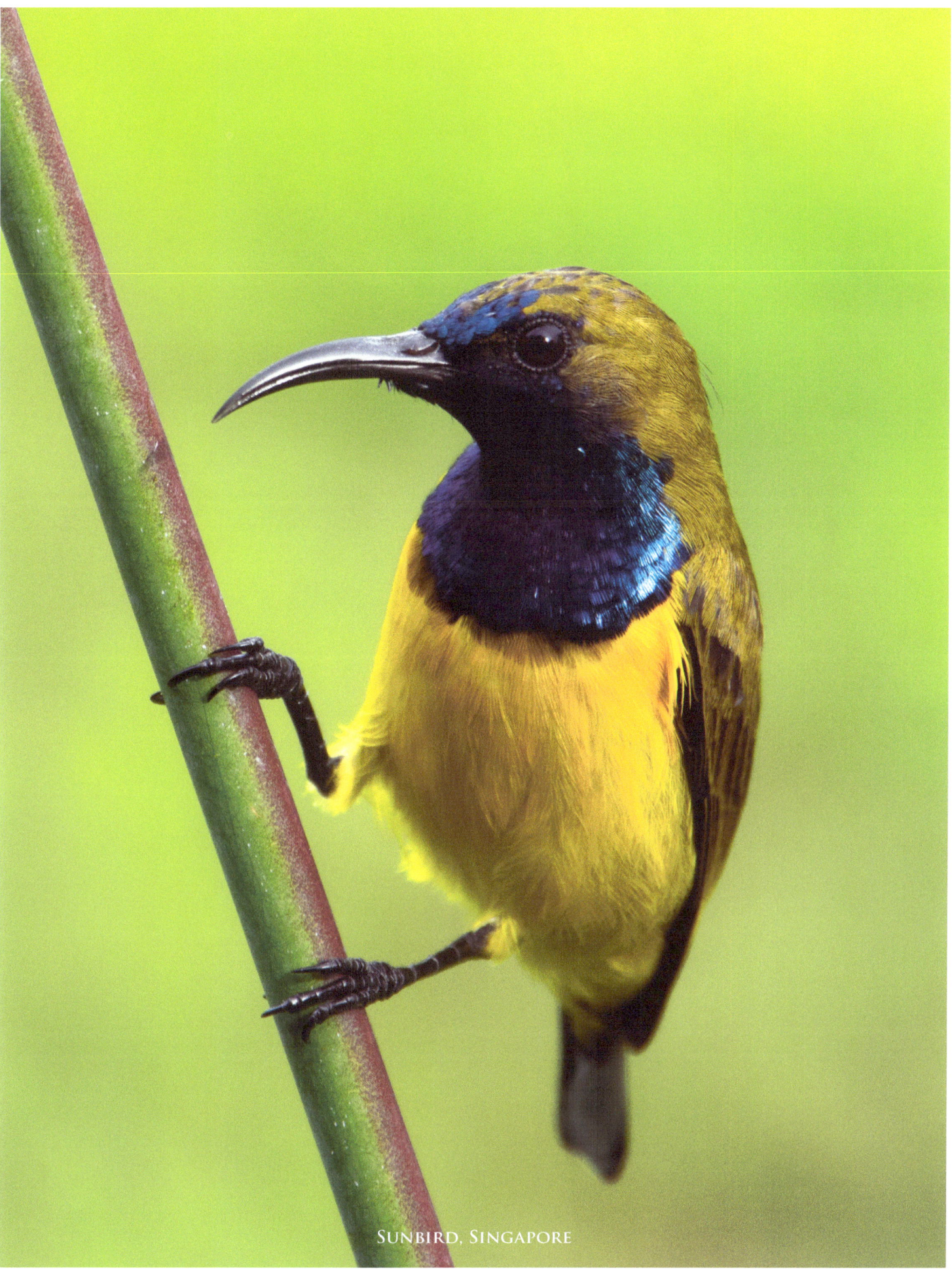

Sunbird, Singapore

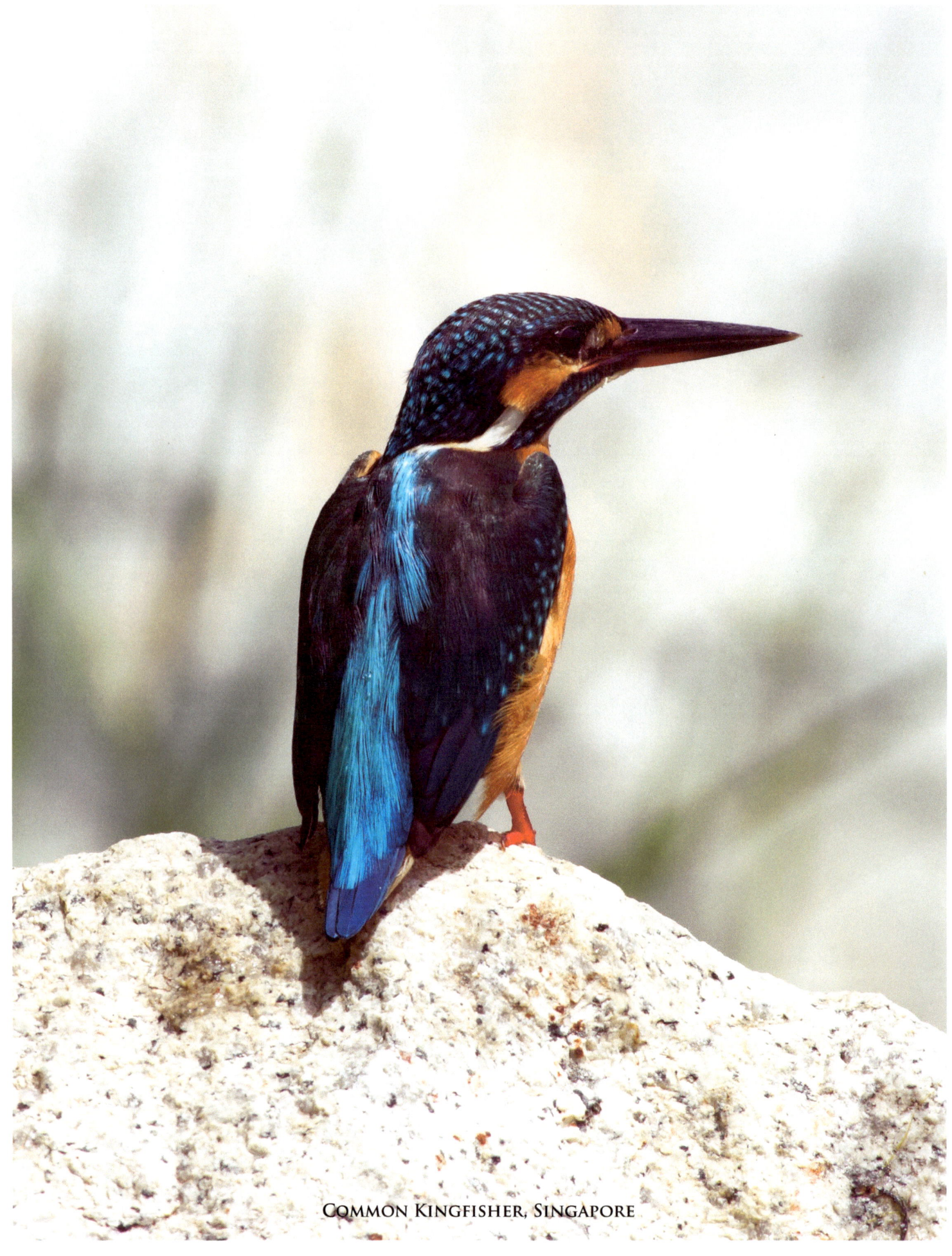

COMMON KINGFISHER, SINGAPORE

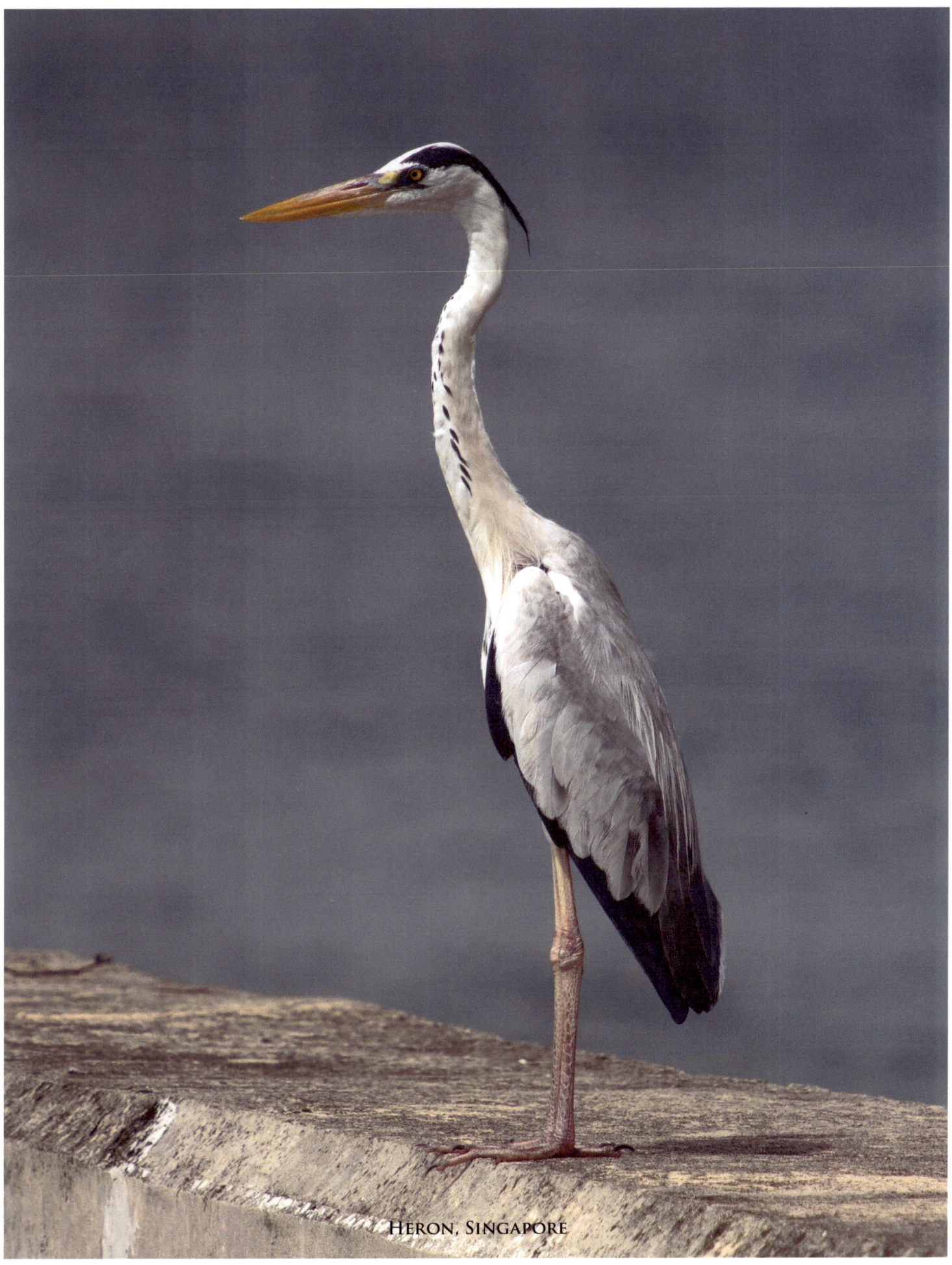

Heron, Singapore

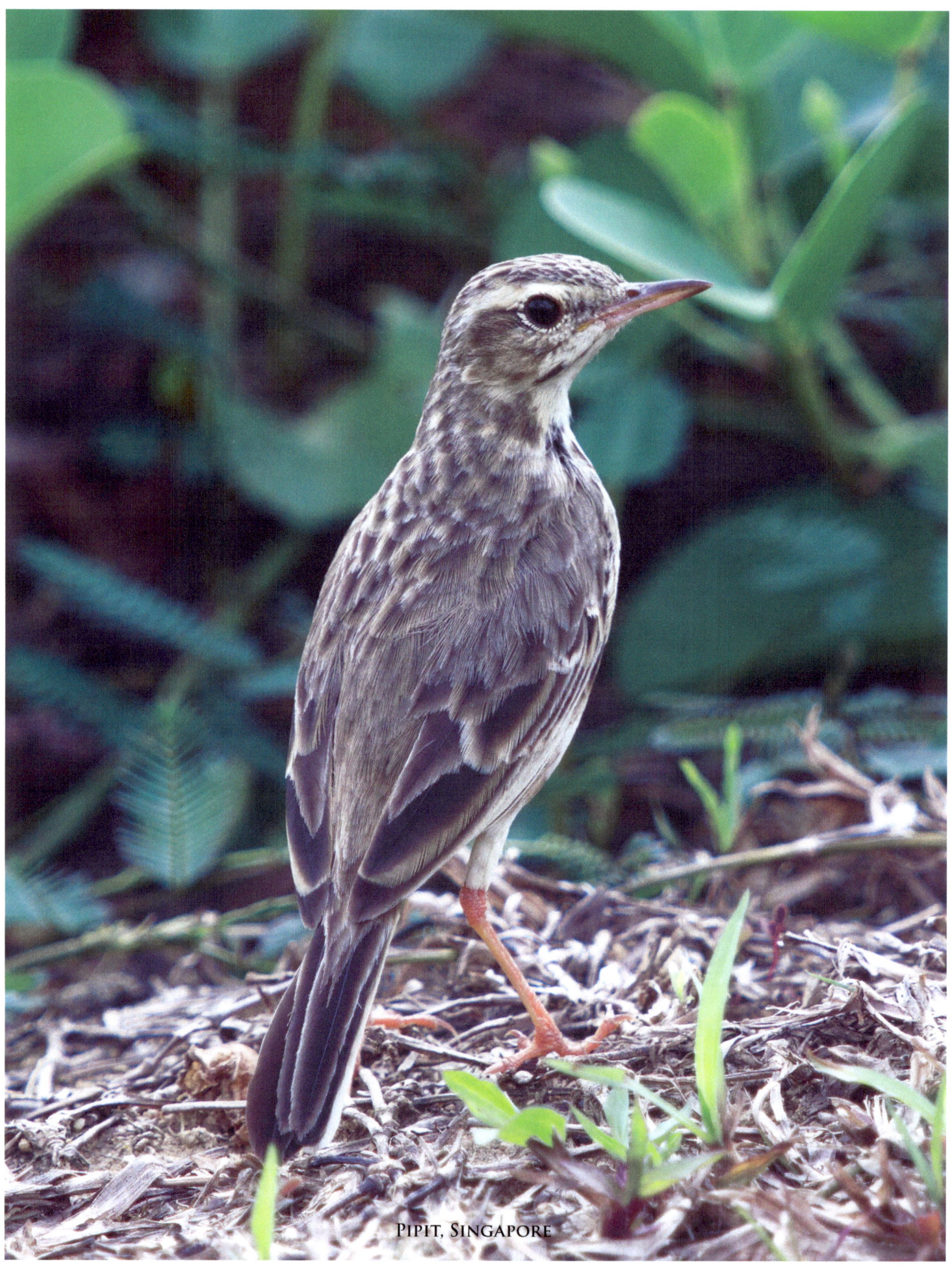

PIPIT, SINGAPORE

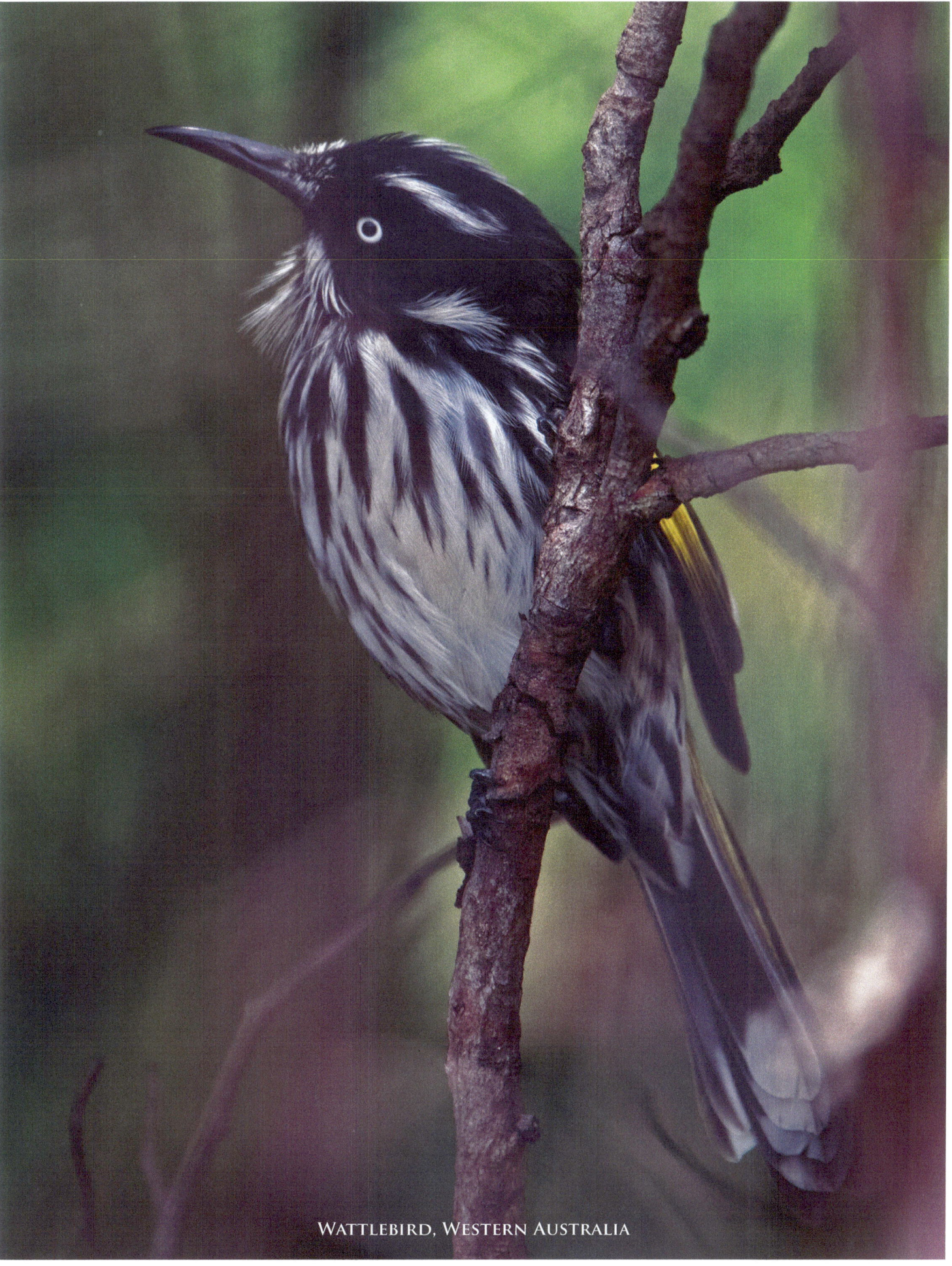

WATTLEBIRD, WESTERN AUSTRALIA

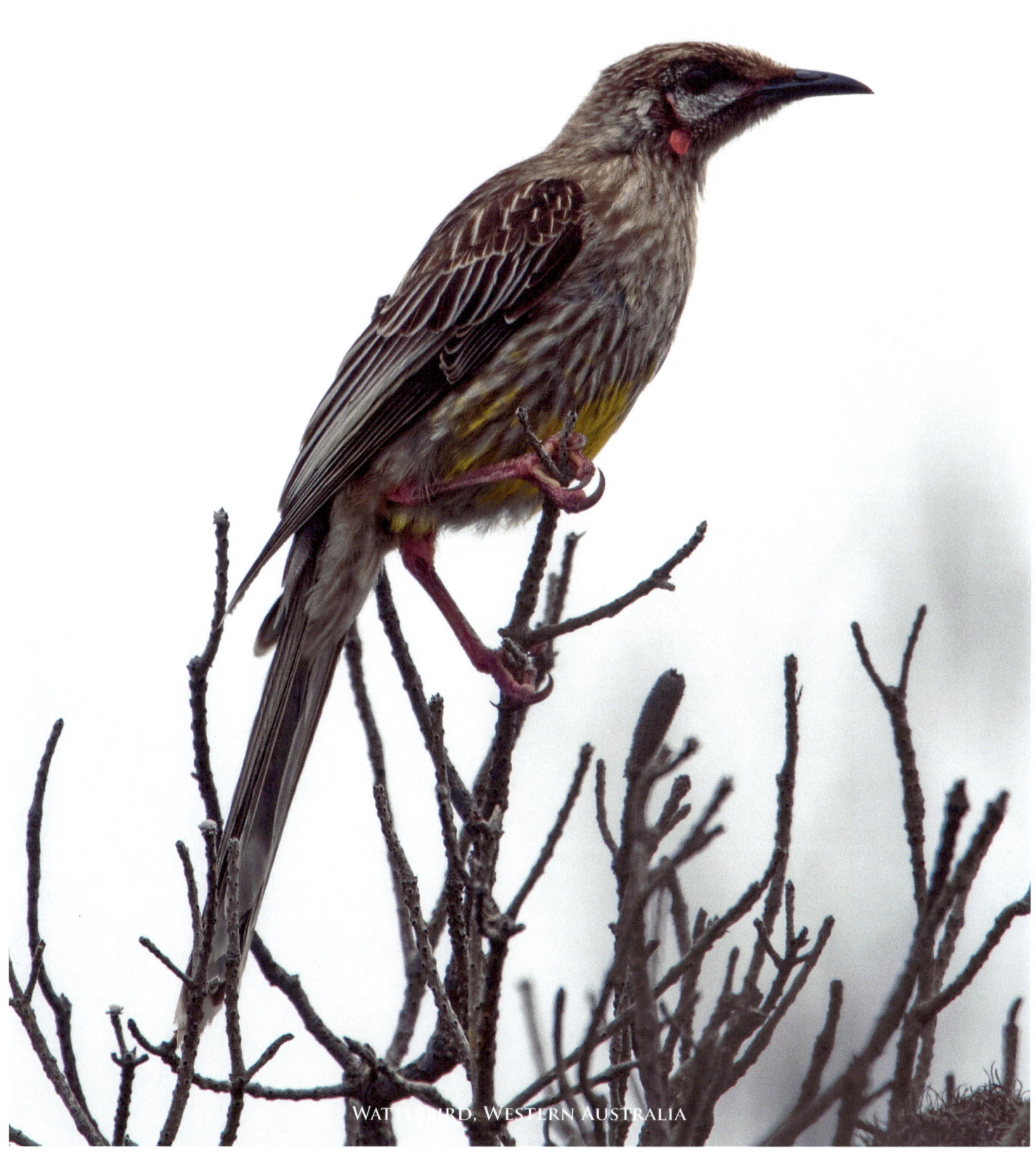

Wattlebird, Western Australia

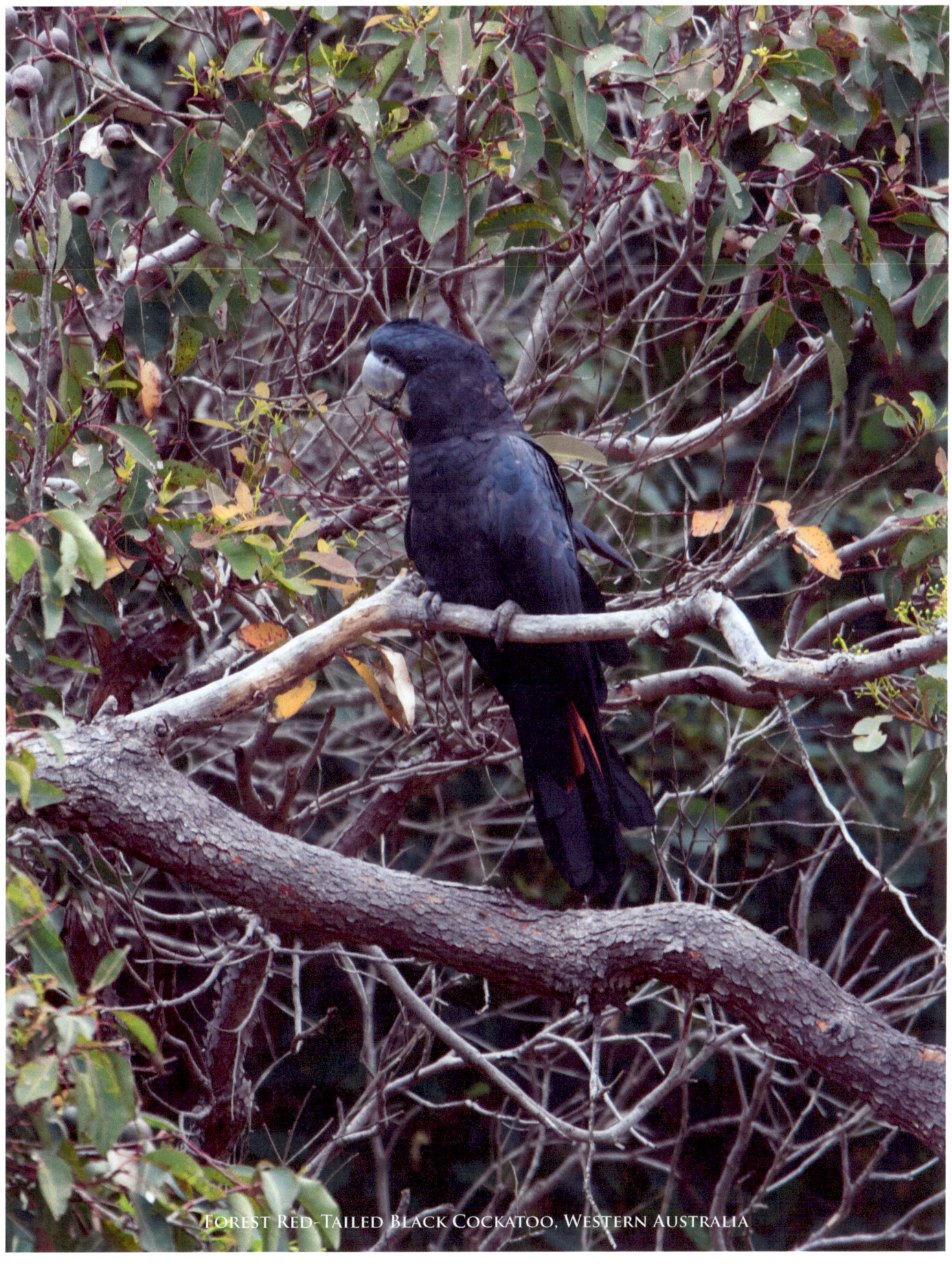

Forest Red-Tailed Black Cockatoo, Western Australia

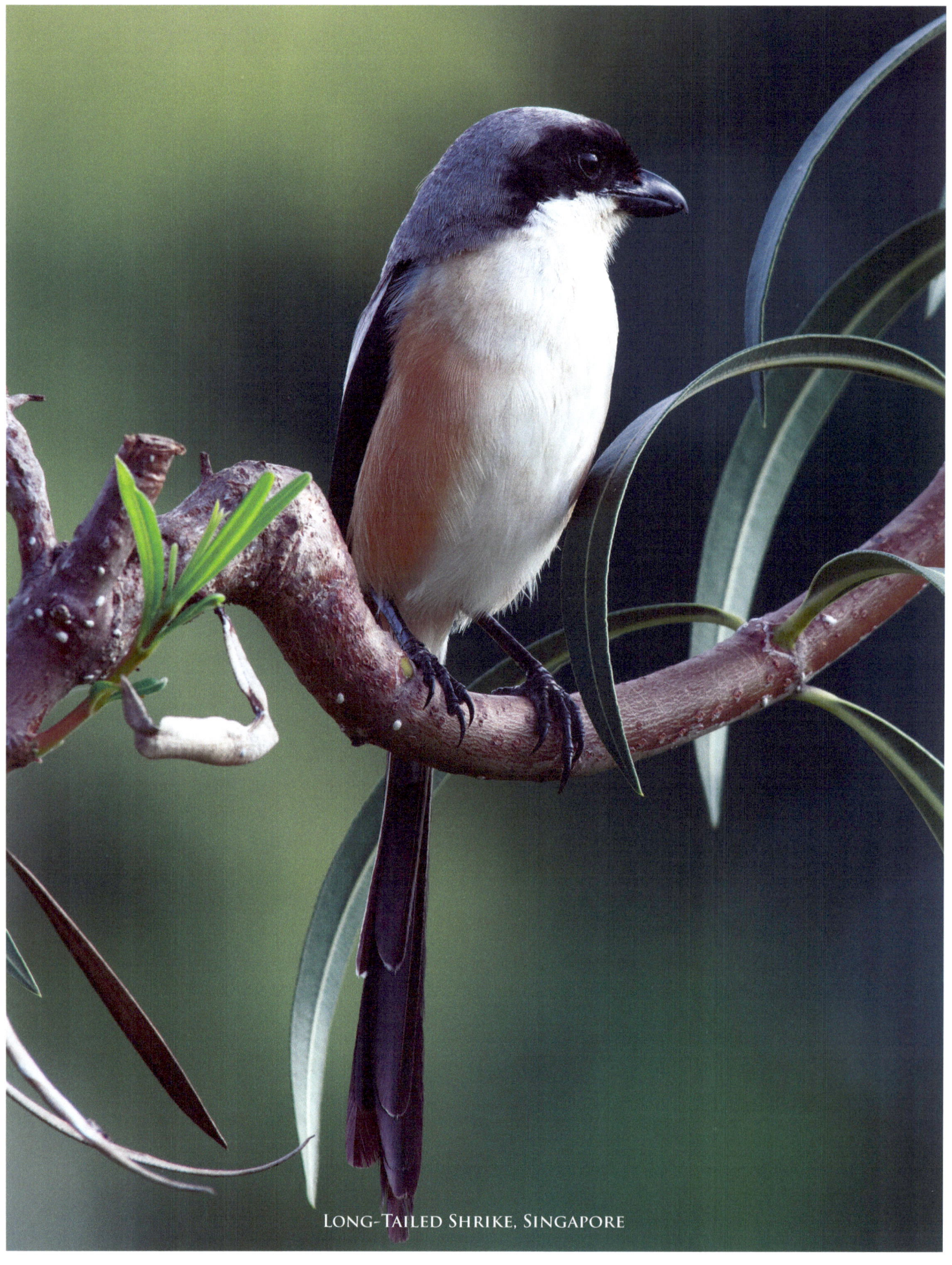

LONG-TAILED SHRIKE, SINGAPORE

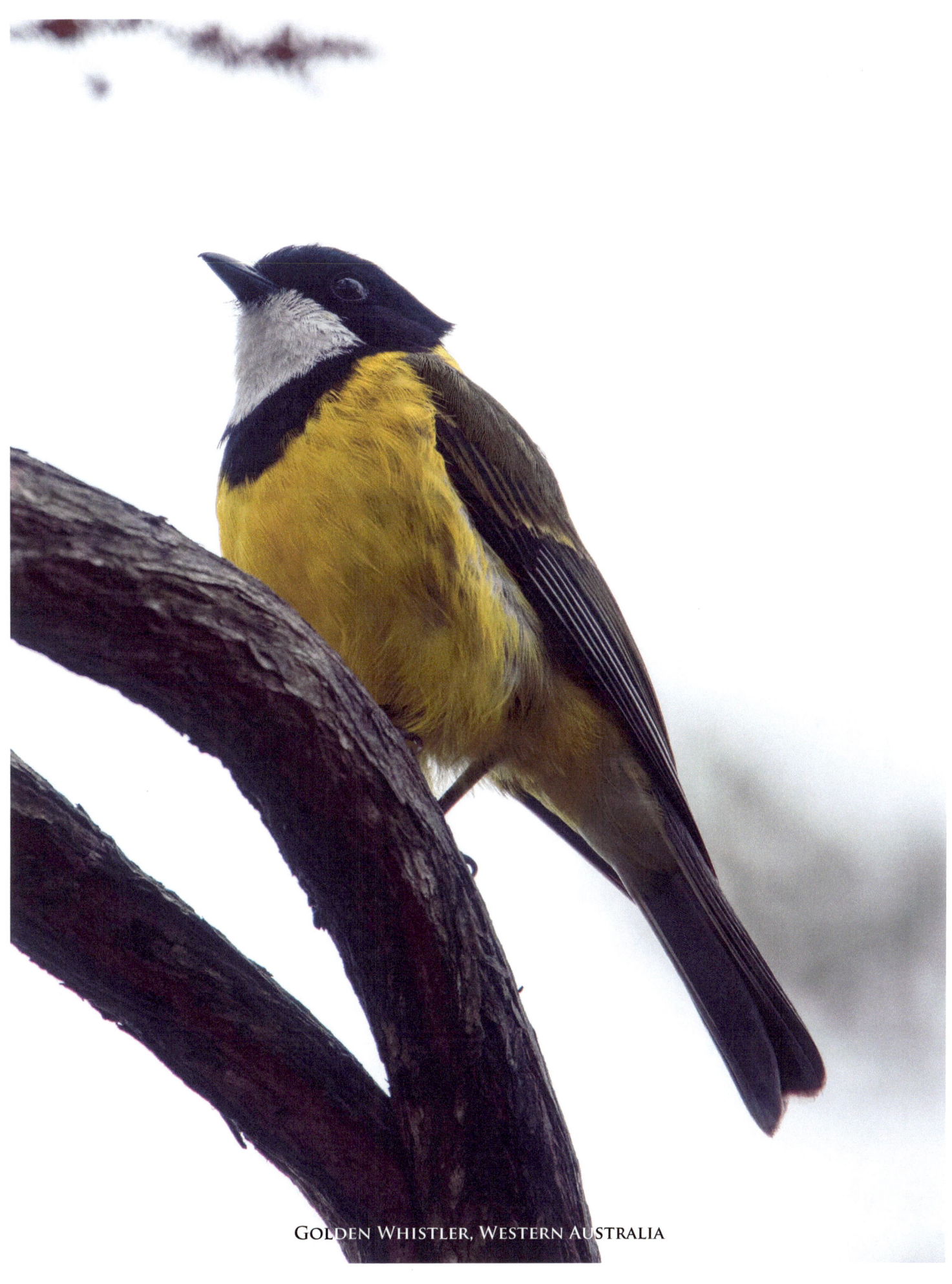

Golden Whistler, Western Australia

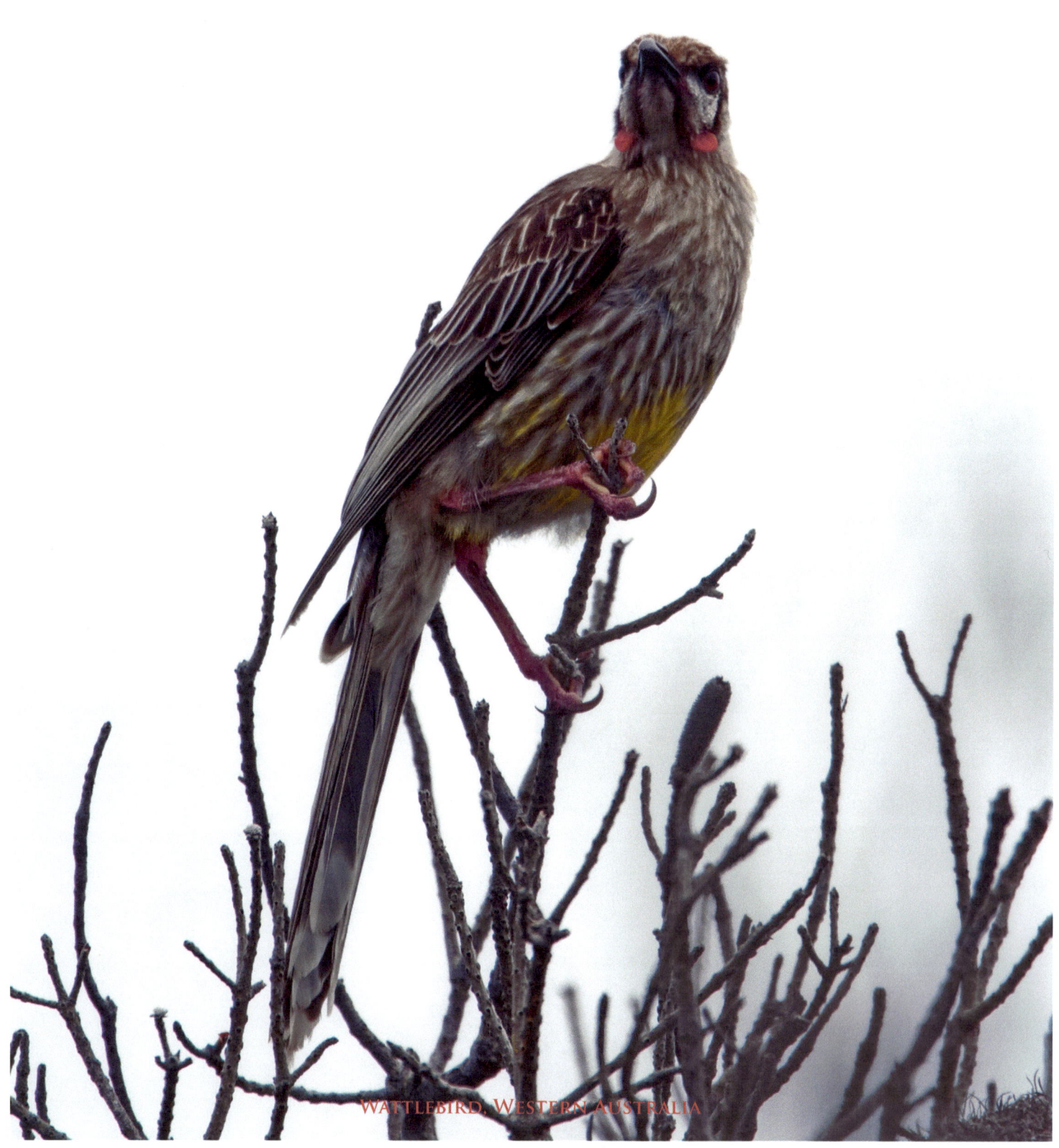

WATTLEBIRD, WESTERN AUSTRALIA

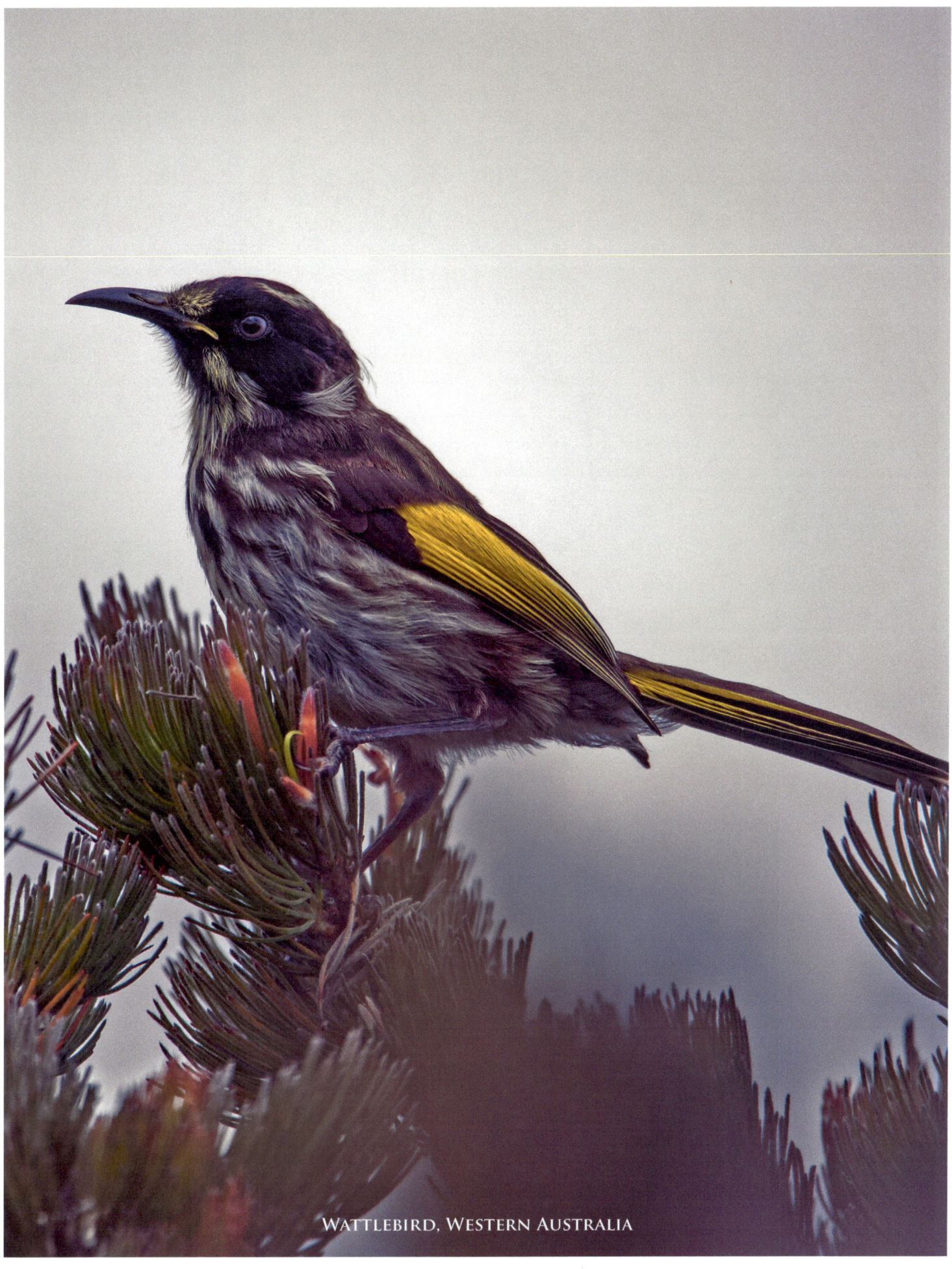

WATTLEBIRD, WESTERN AUSTRALIA

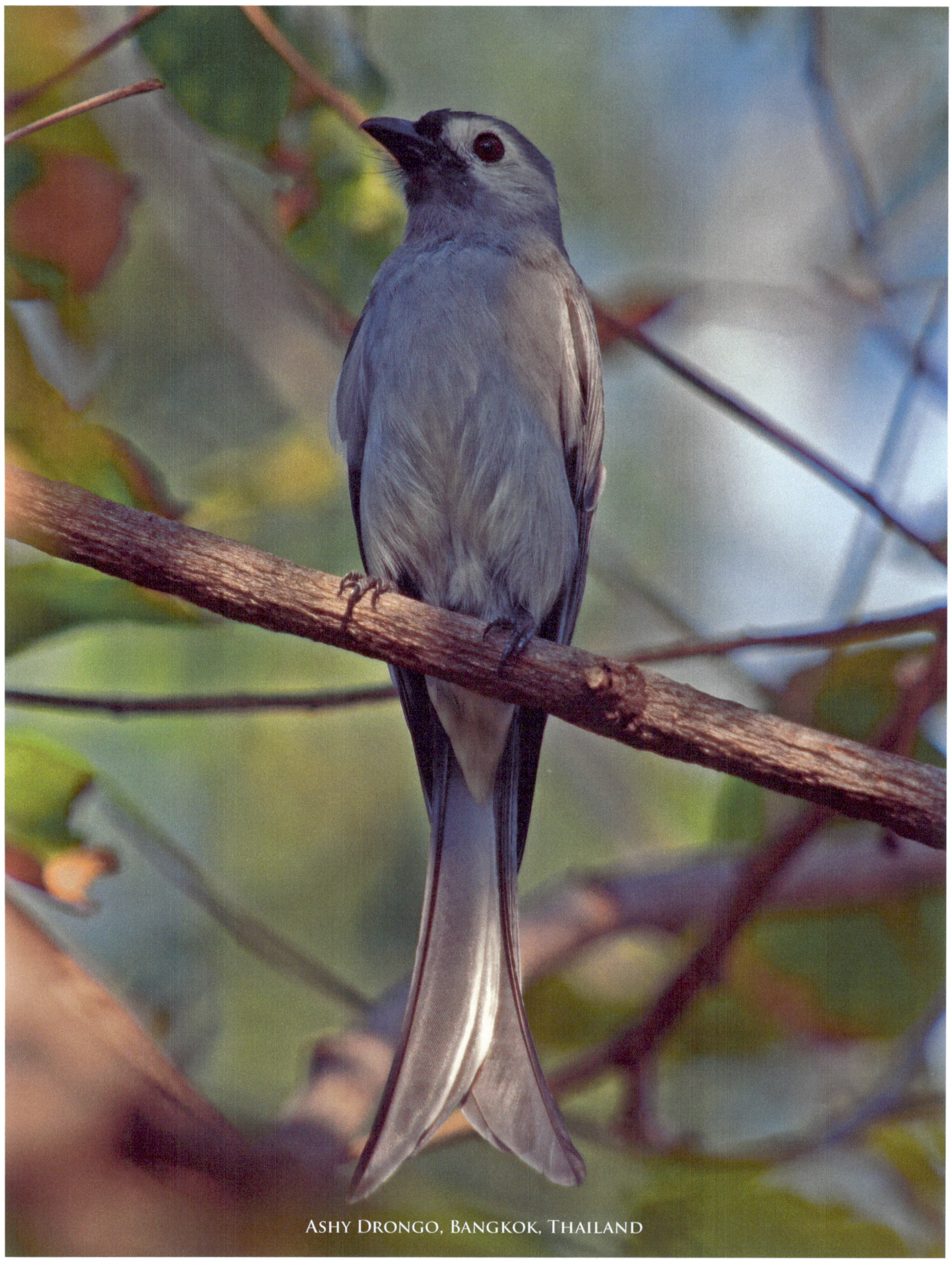

ASHY DRONGO, BANGKOK, THAILAND

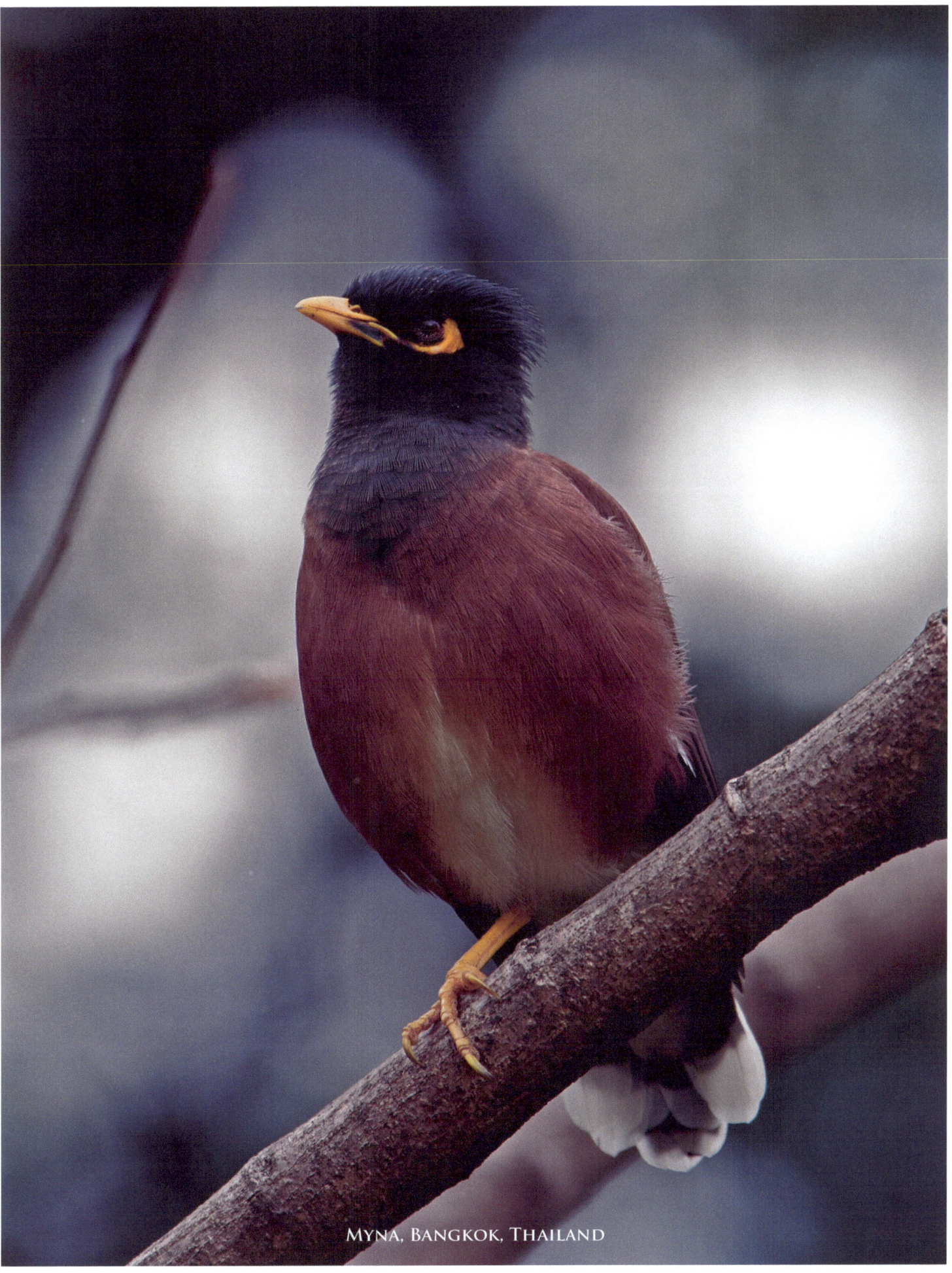

MYNA, BANGKOK, THAILAND

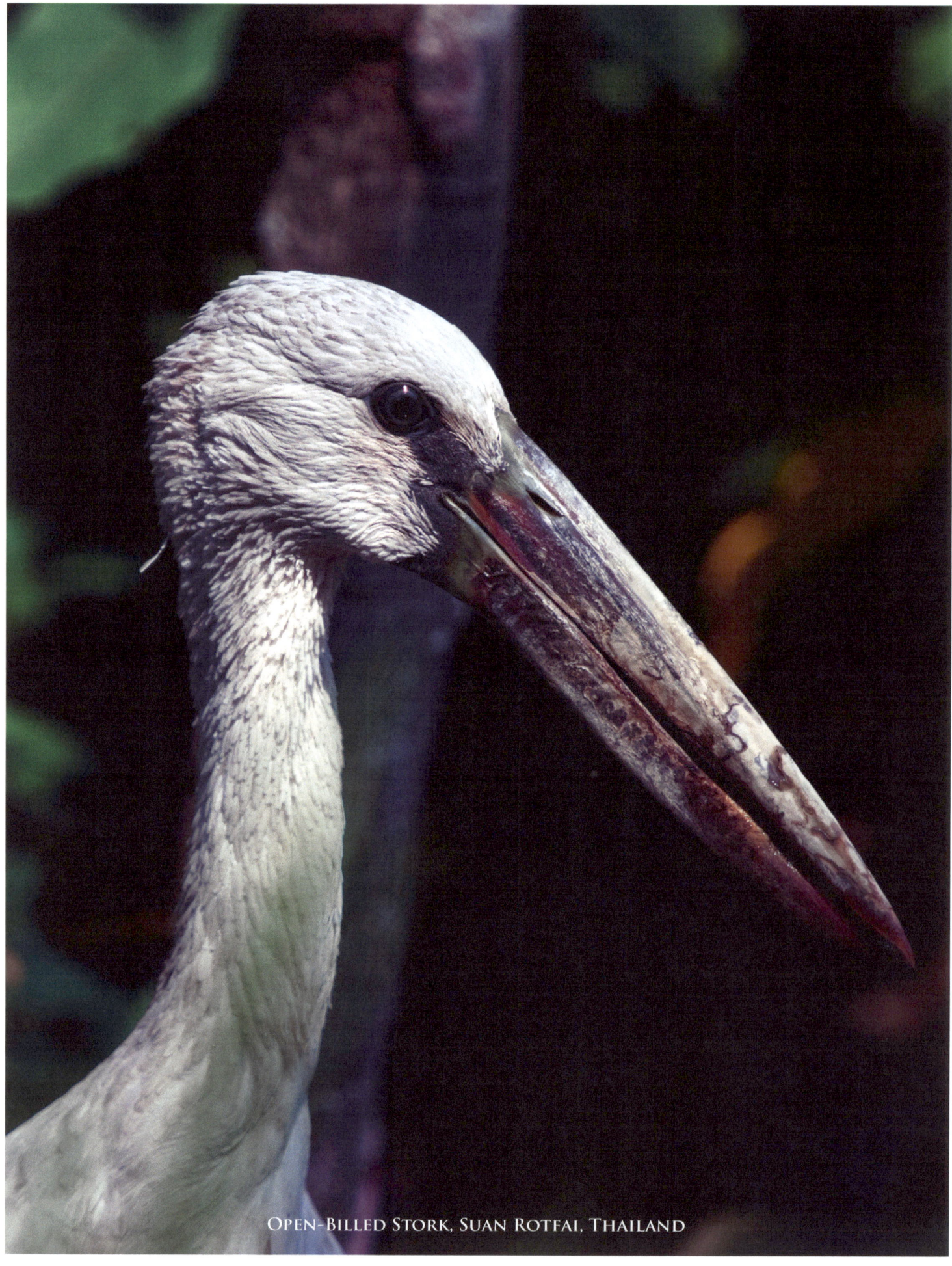

OPEN-BILLED STORK, SUAN ROTFAI, THAILAND

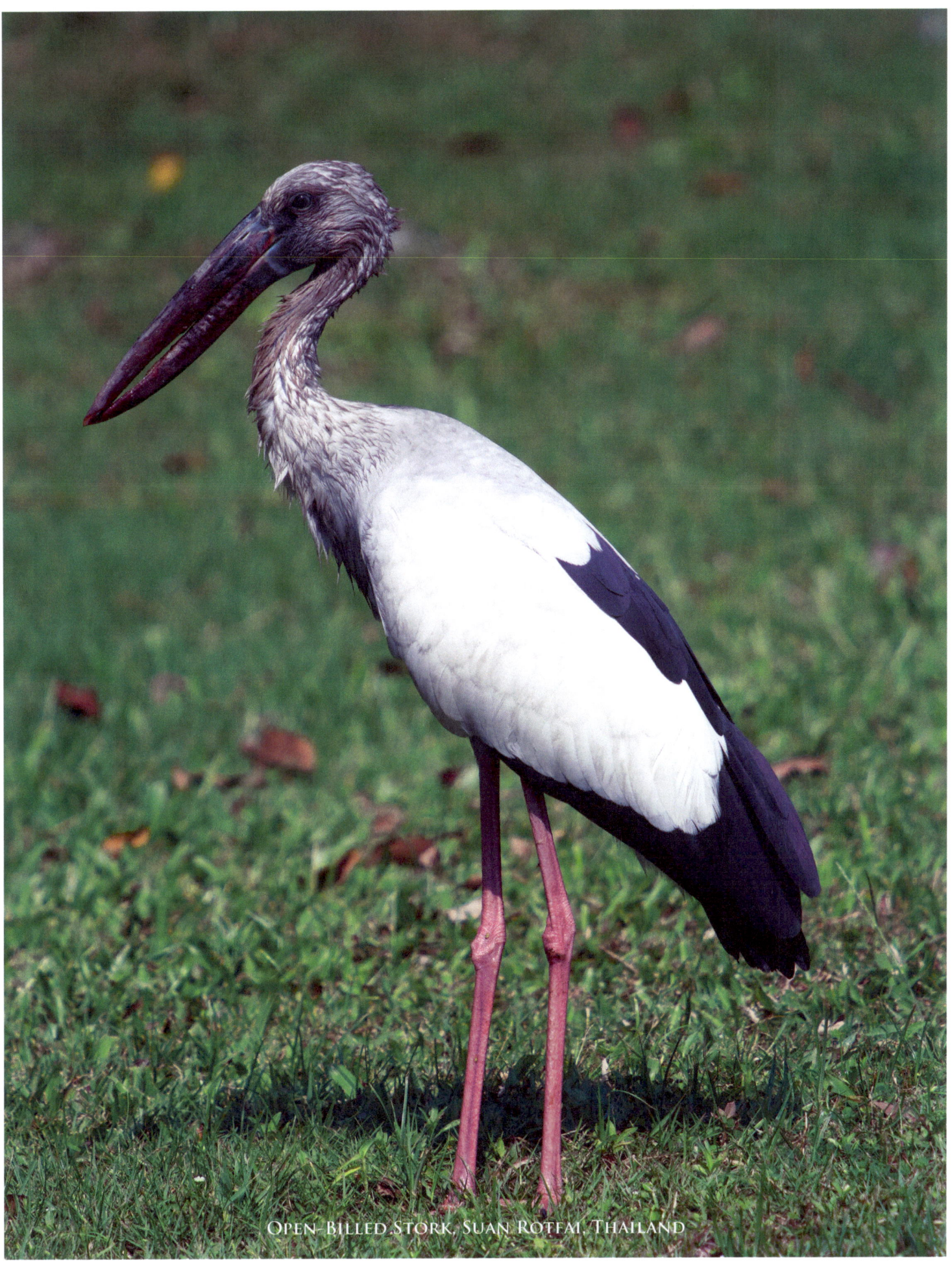

OPEN-BILLED STORK, SUAN ROTFAI, THAILAND

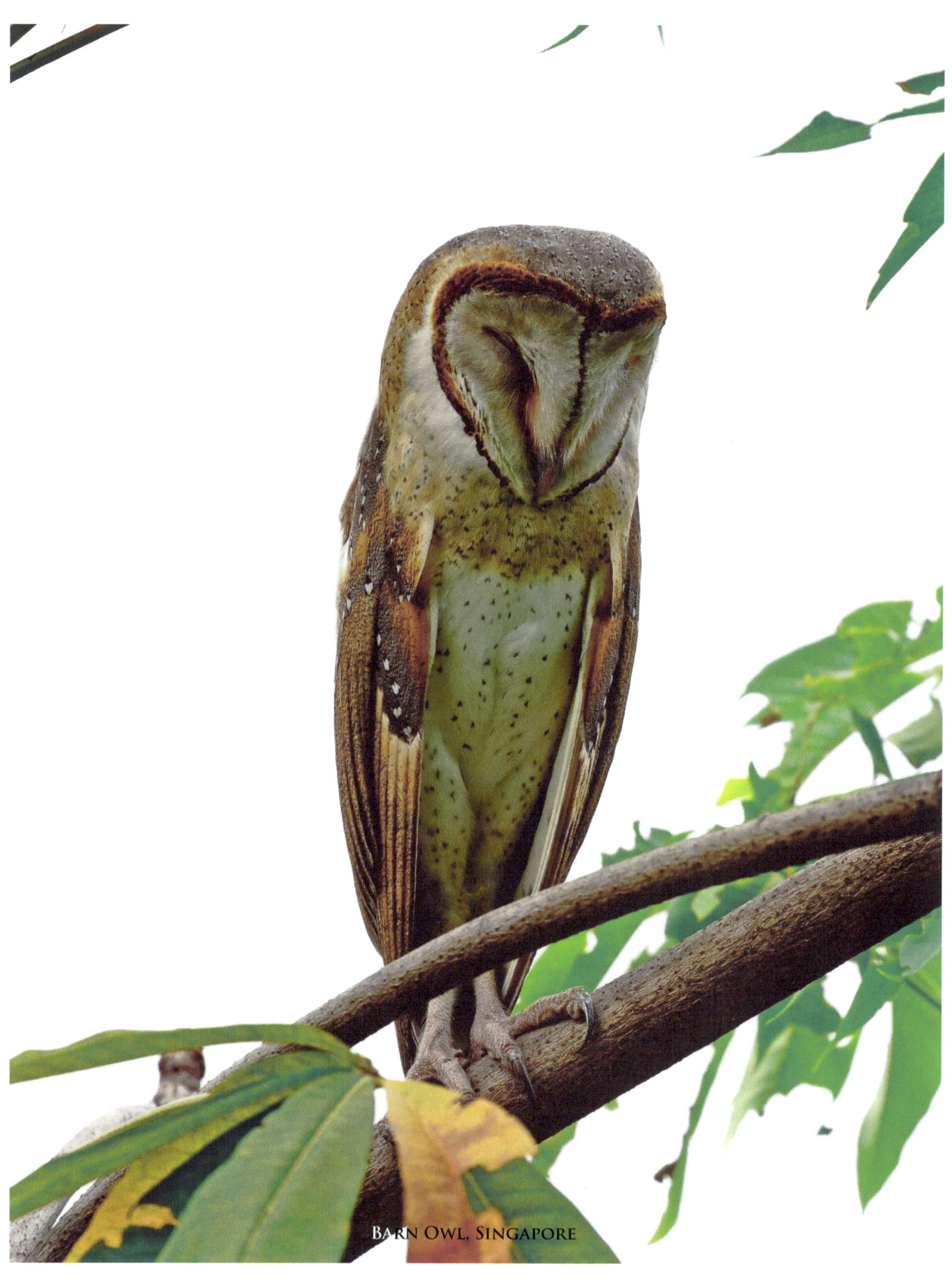

Barn Owl, Singapore

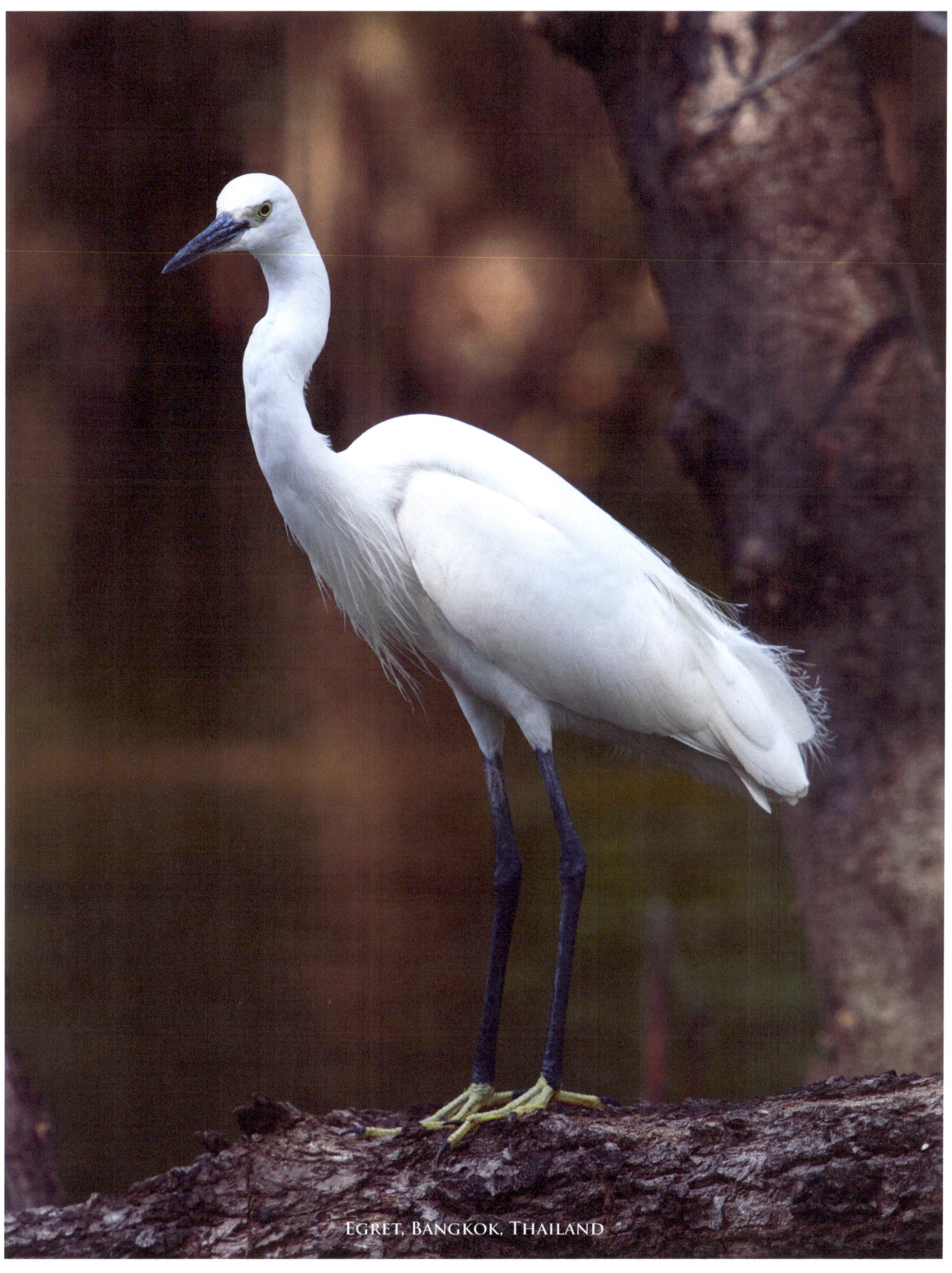

EGRET, BANGKOK, THAILAND

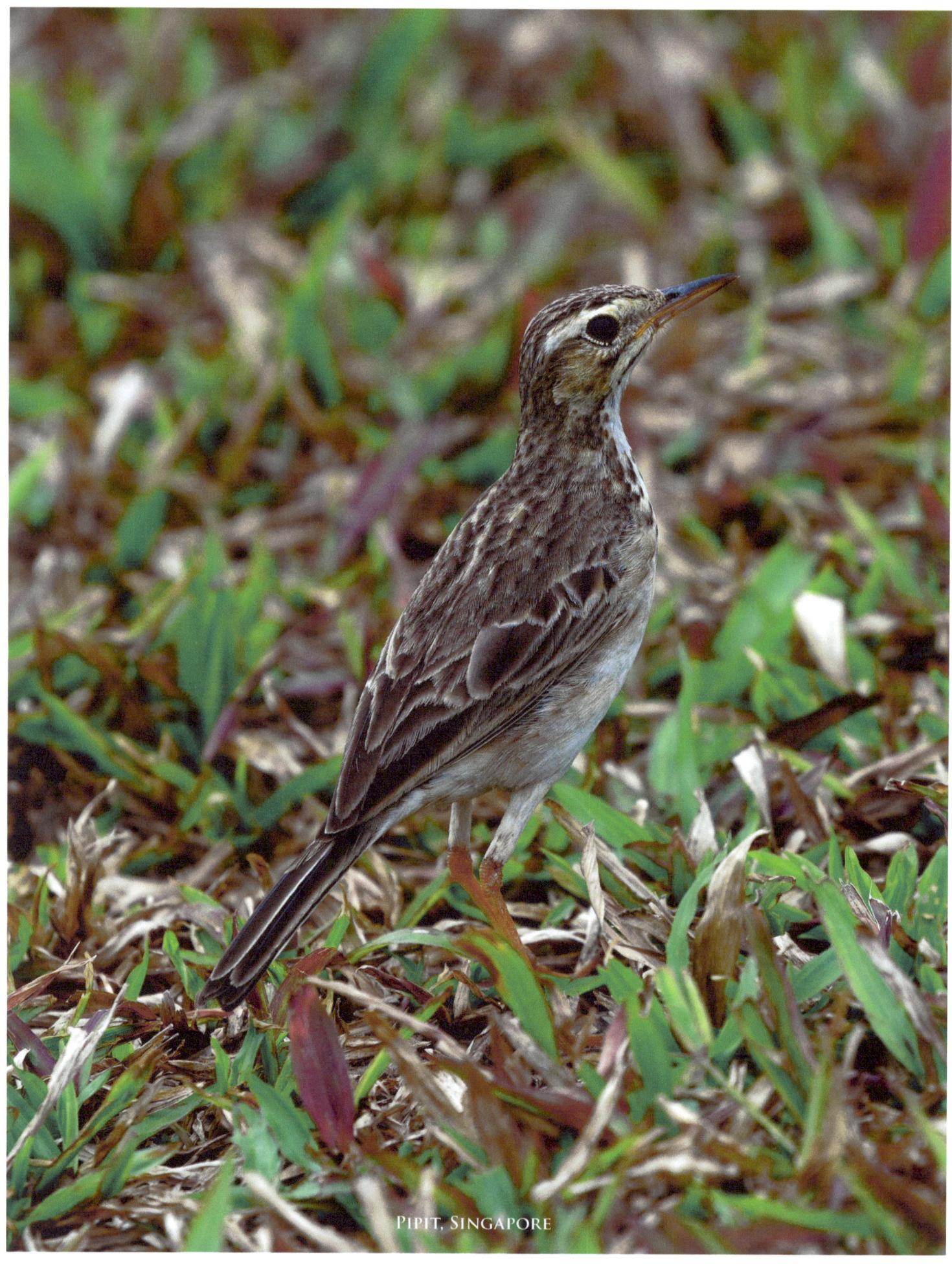

PIPIT, SINGAPORE

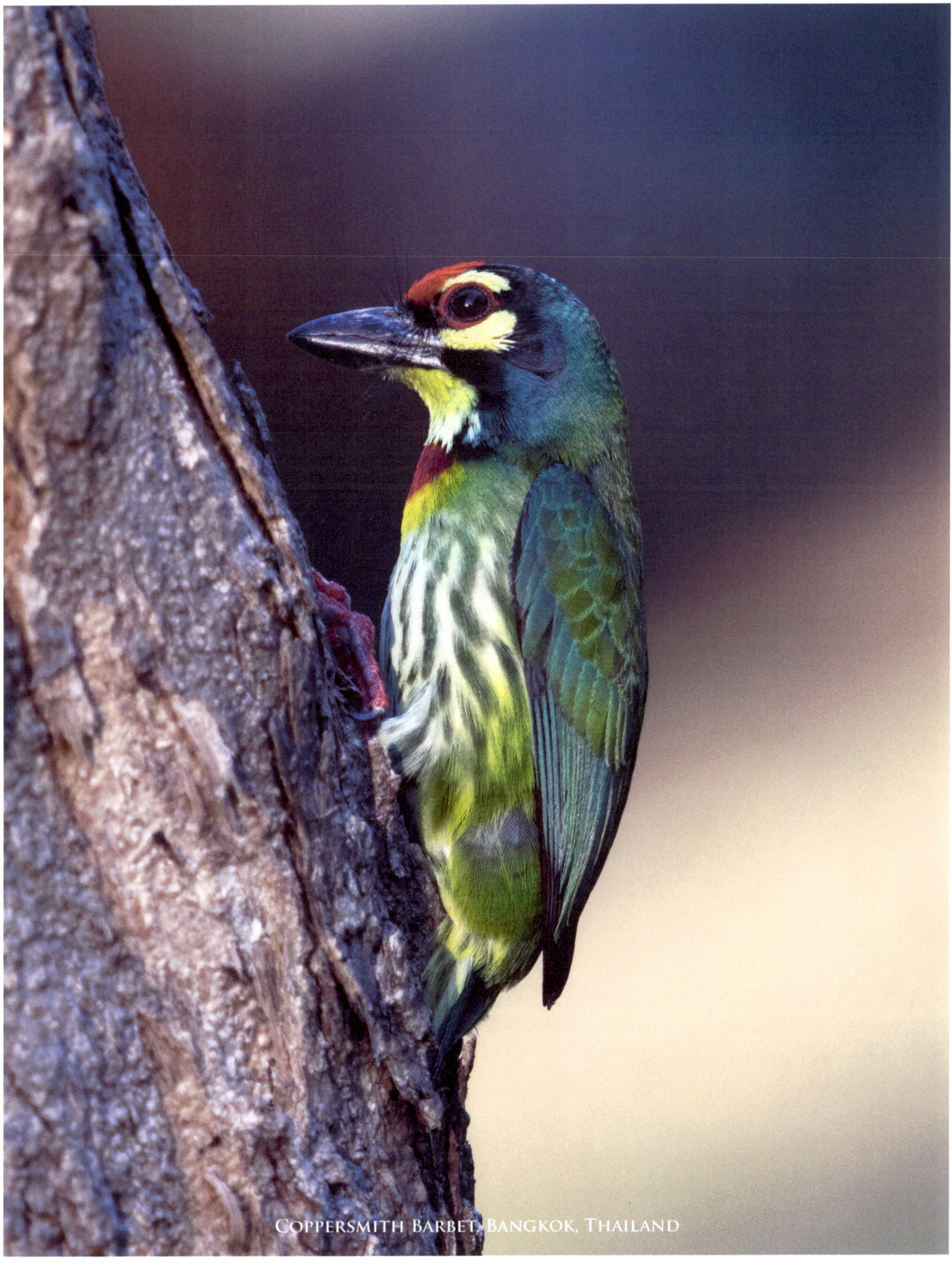
Coppersmith Barbet, Bangkok, Thailand

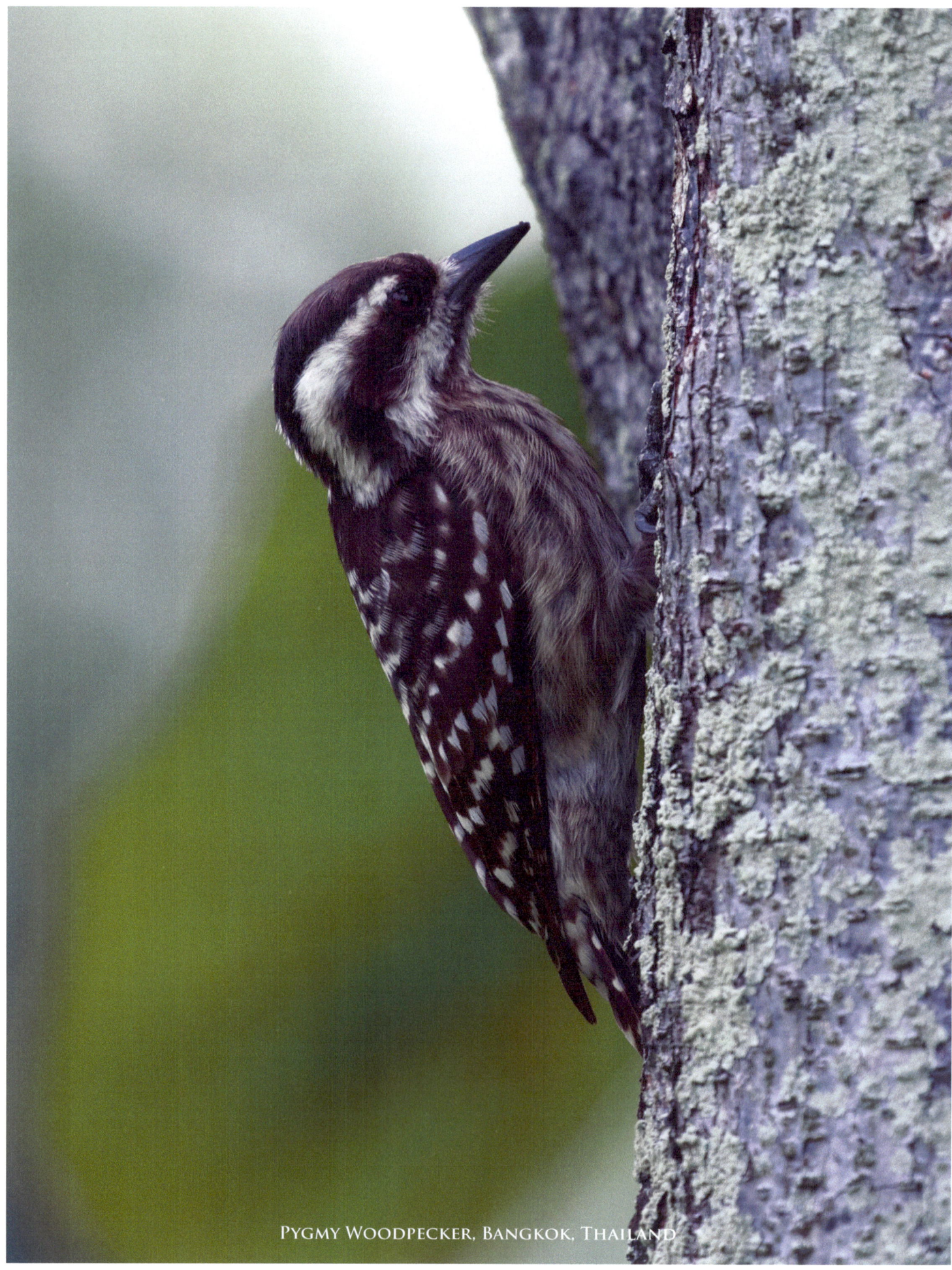

PYGMY WOODPECKER, BANGKOK, THAILAND

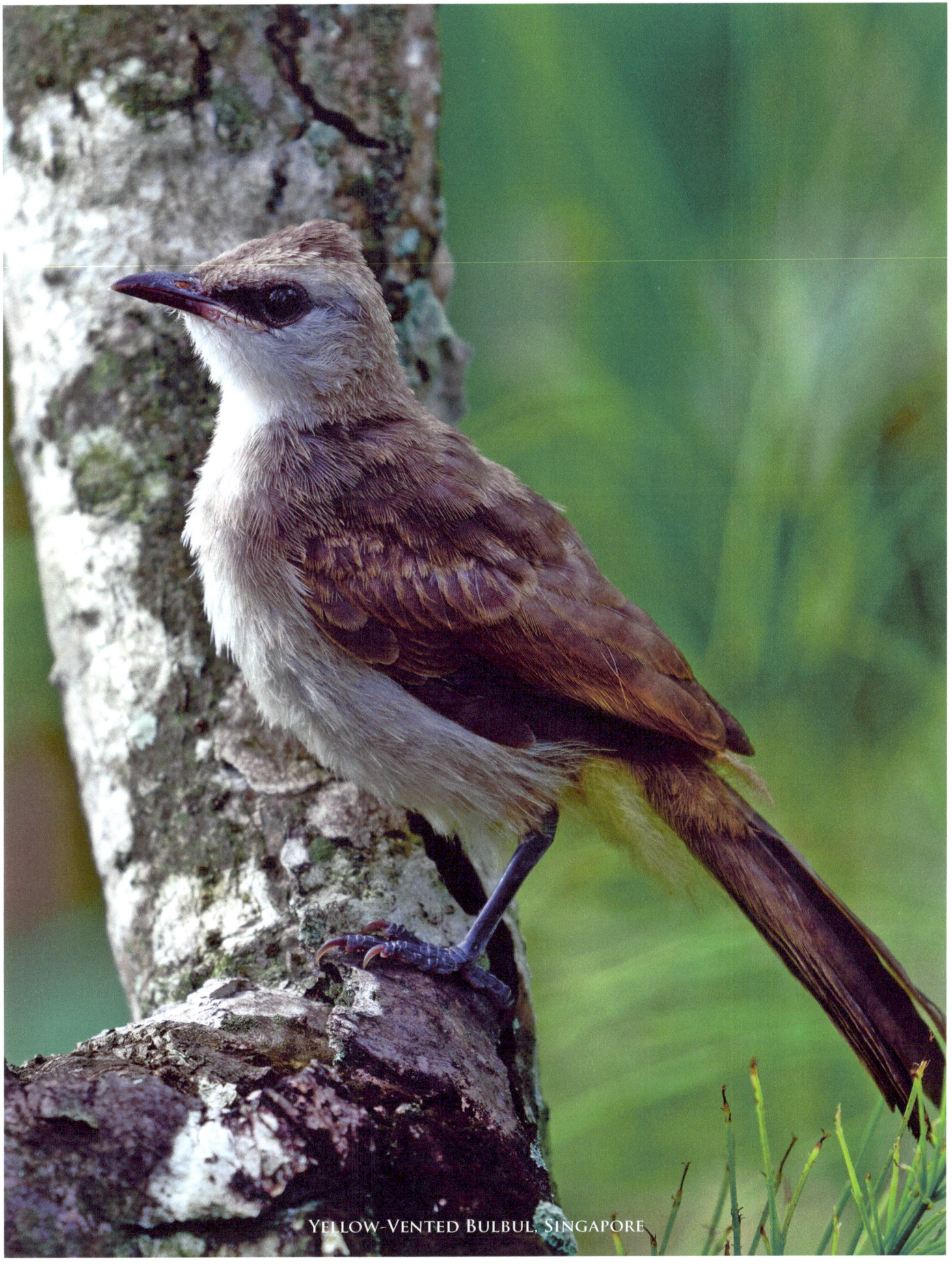

YELLOW-VENTED BULBUL, SINGAPORE

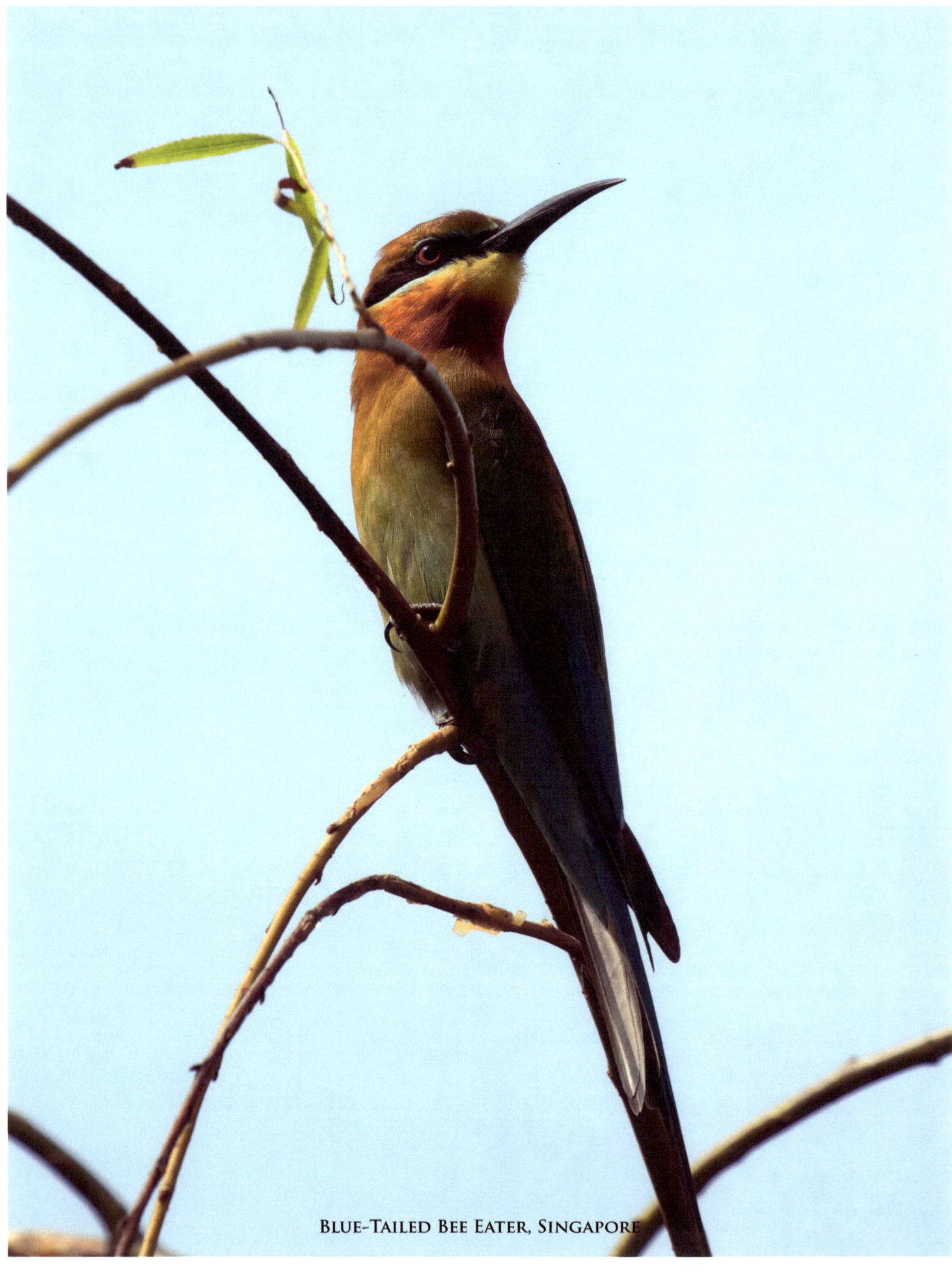

BLUE-TAILED BEE EATER, SINGAPORE

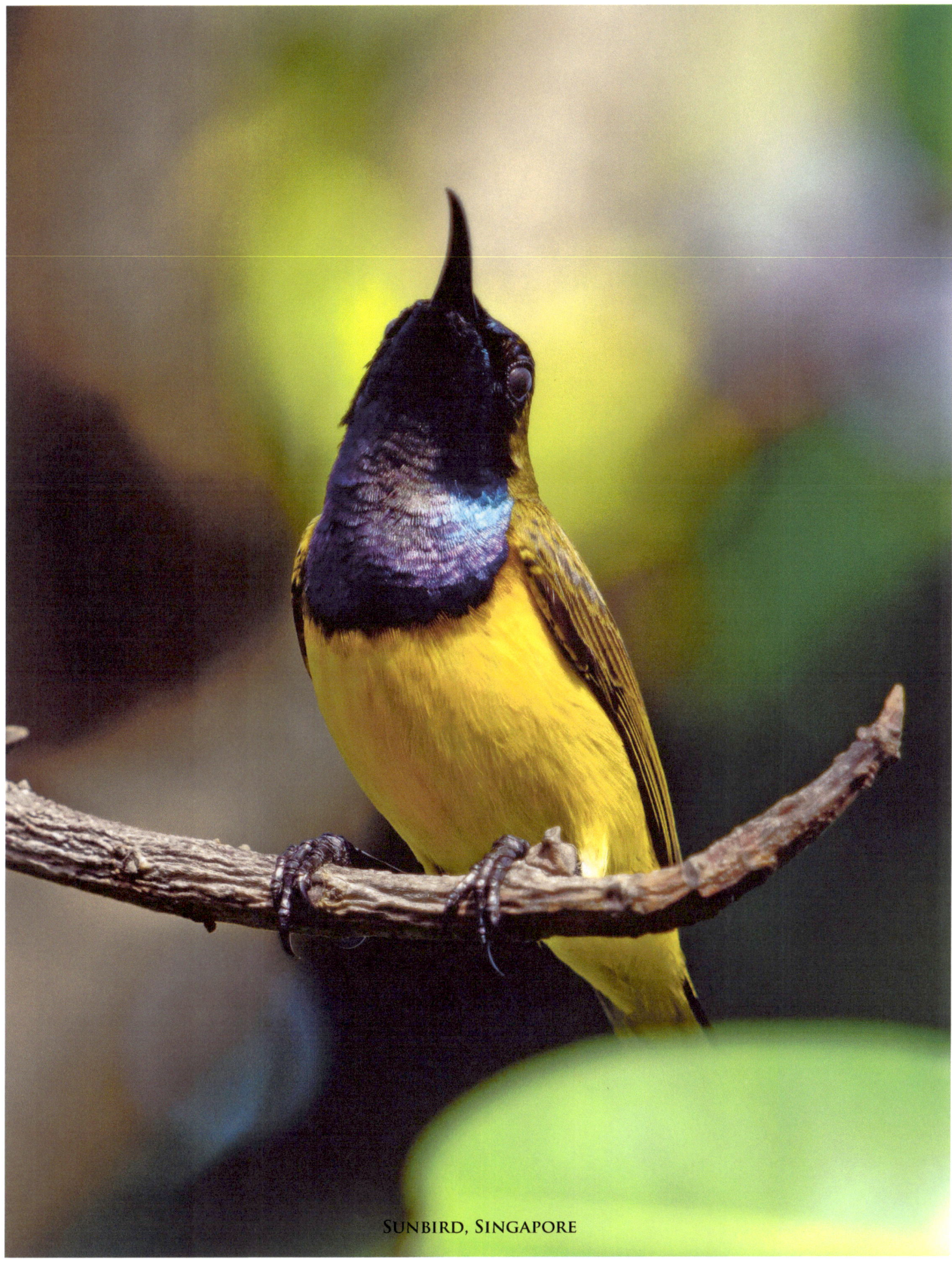

Sunbird, Singapore

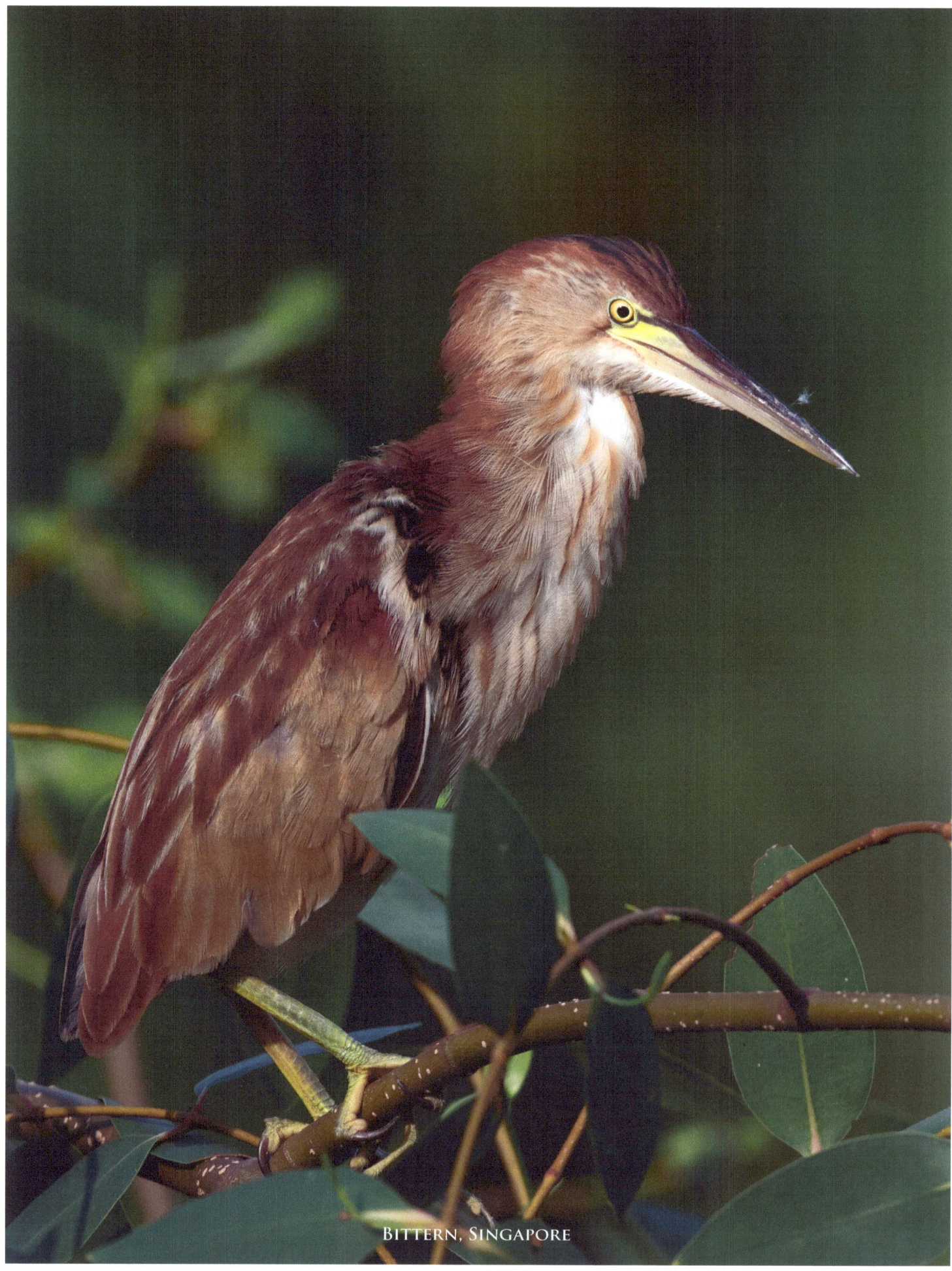

BITTERN, SINGAPORE

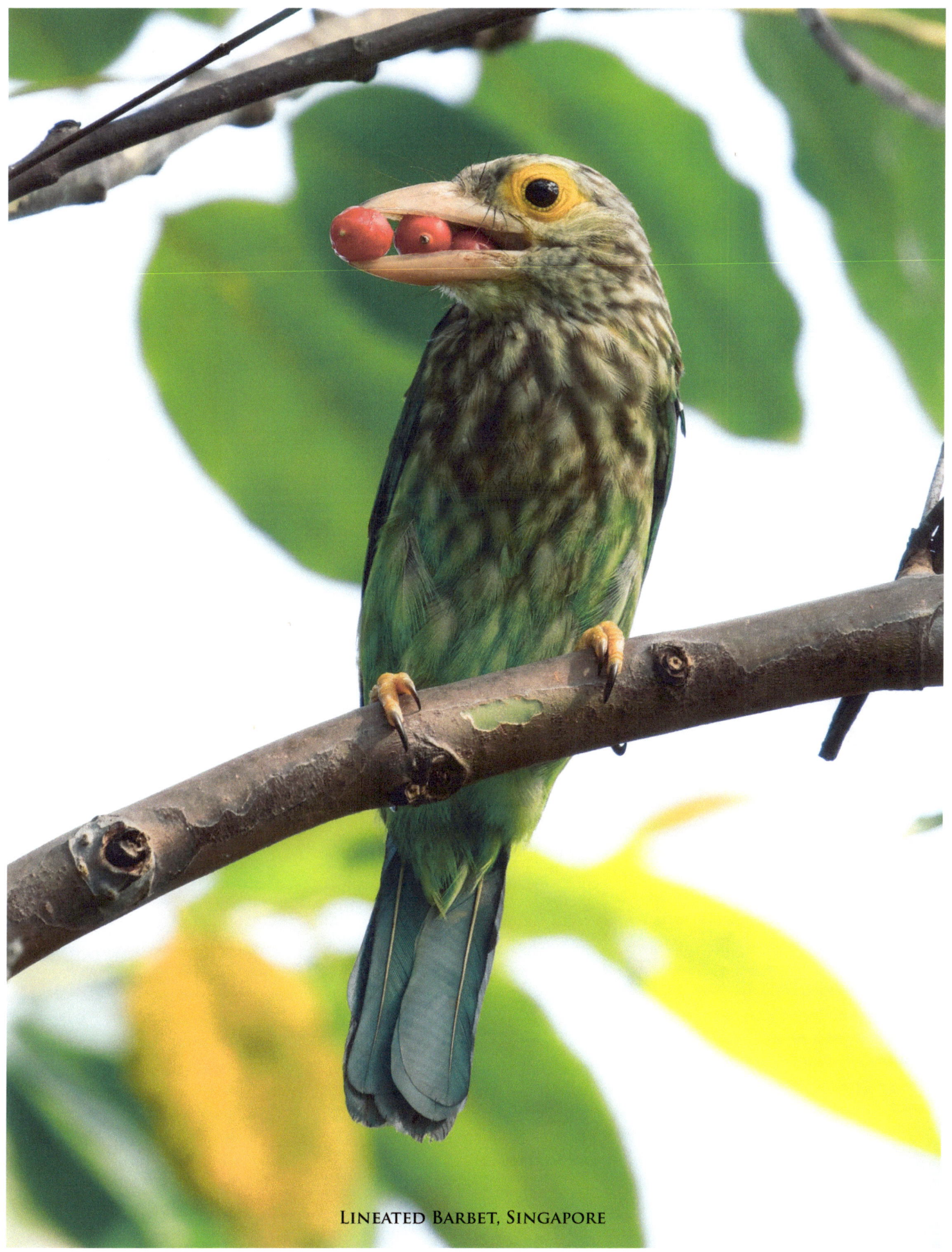

LINEATED BARBET, SINGAPORE

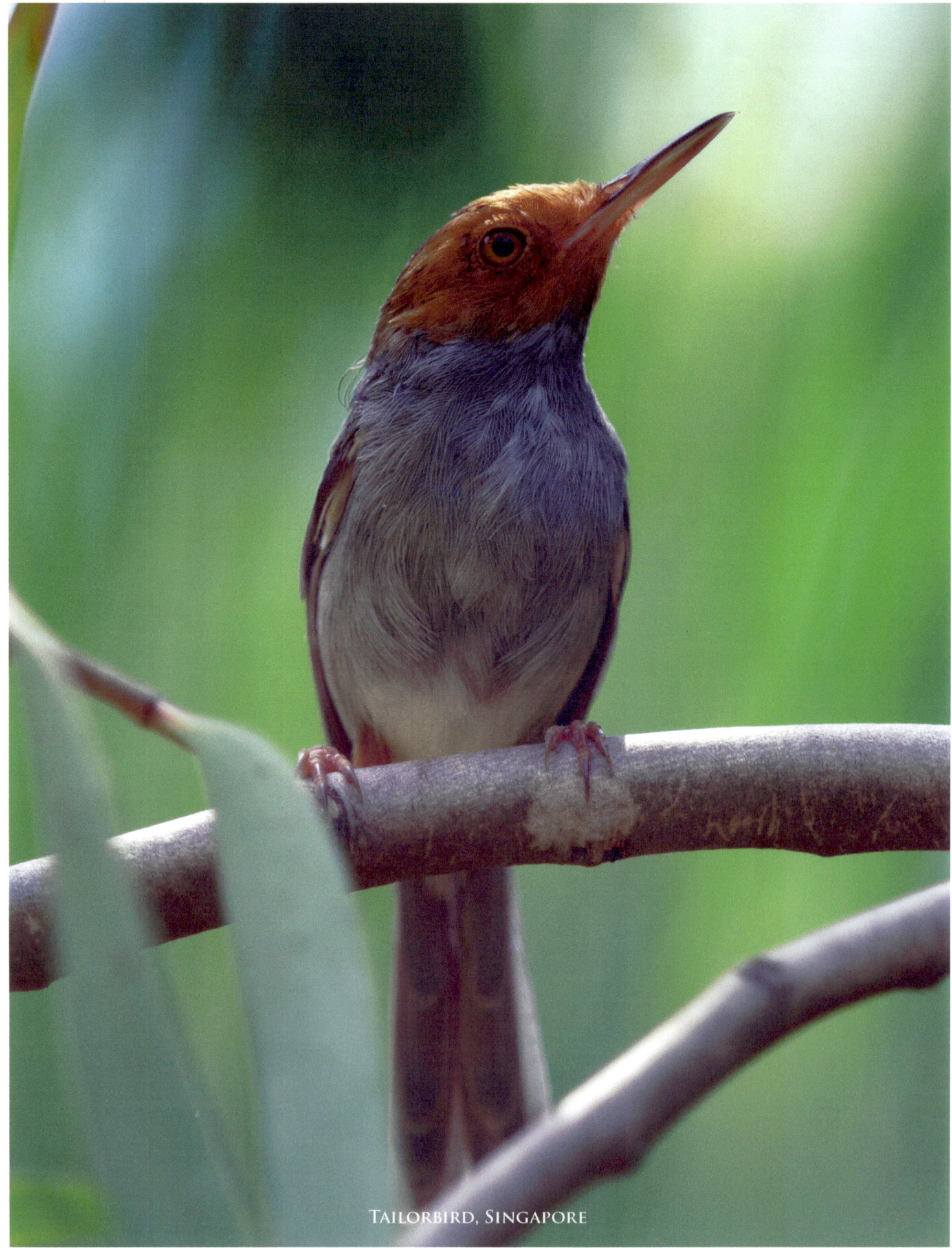

TAILORBIRD, SINGAPORE

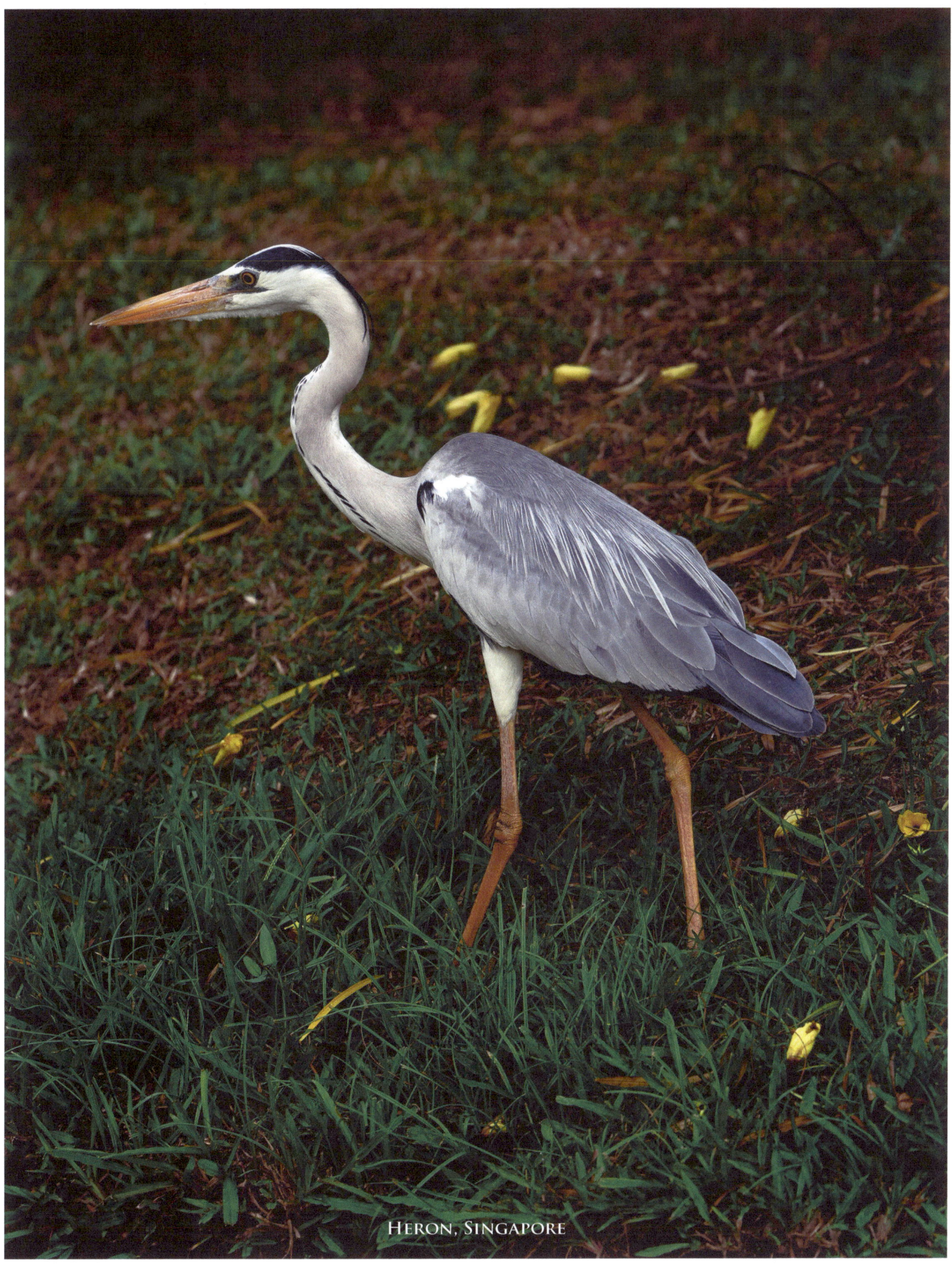

HERON, SINGAPORE

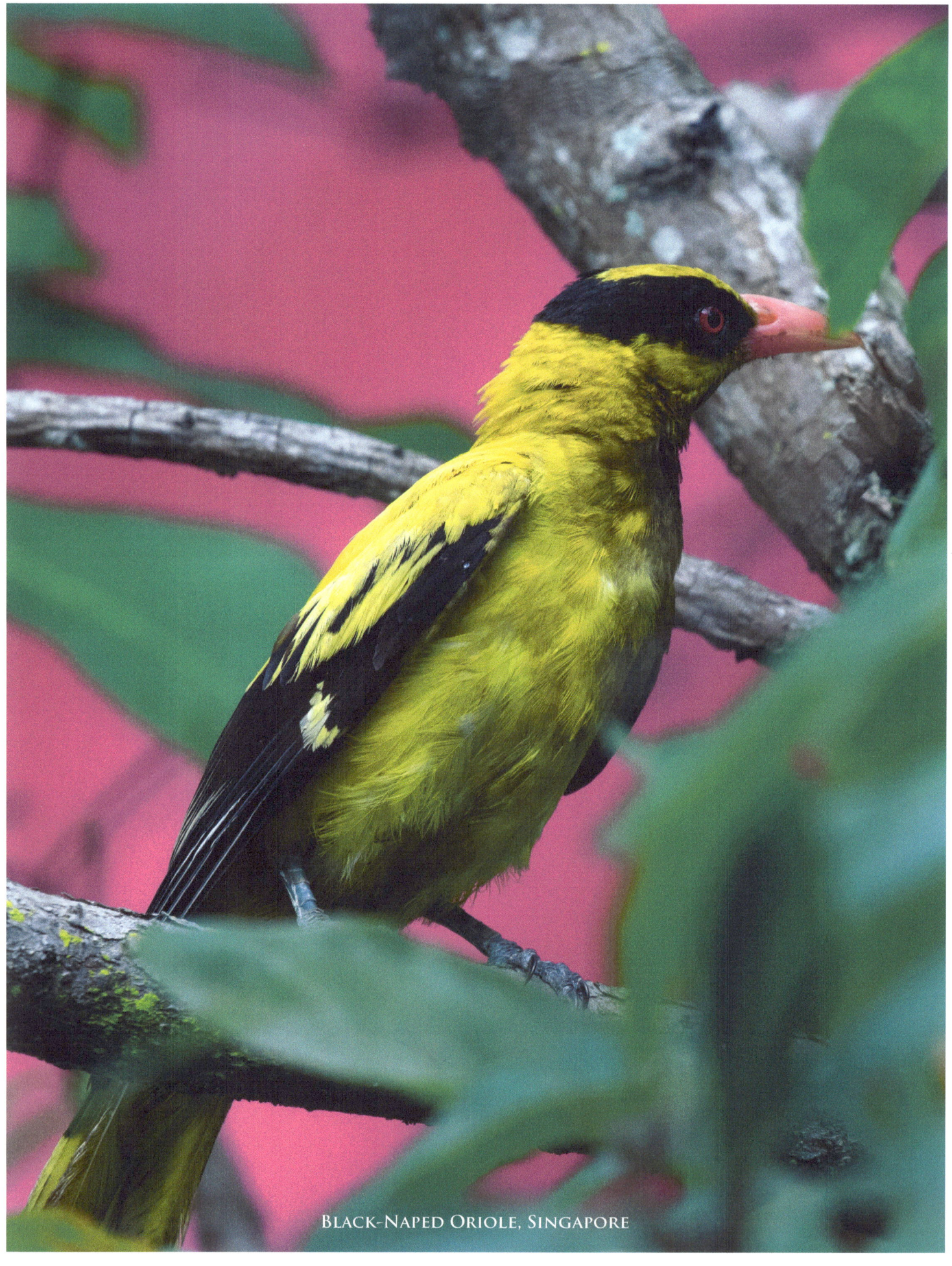

BLACK-NAPED ORIOLE, SINGAPORE

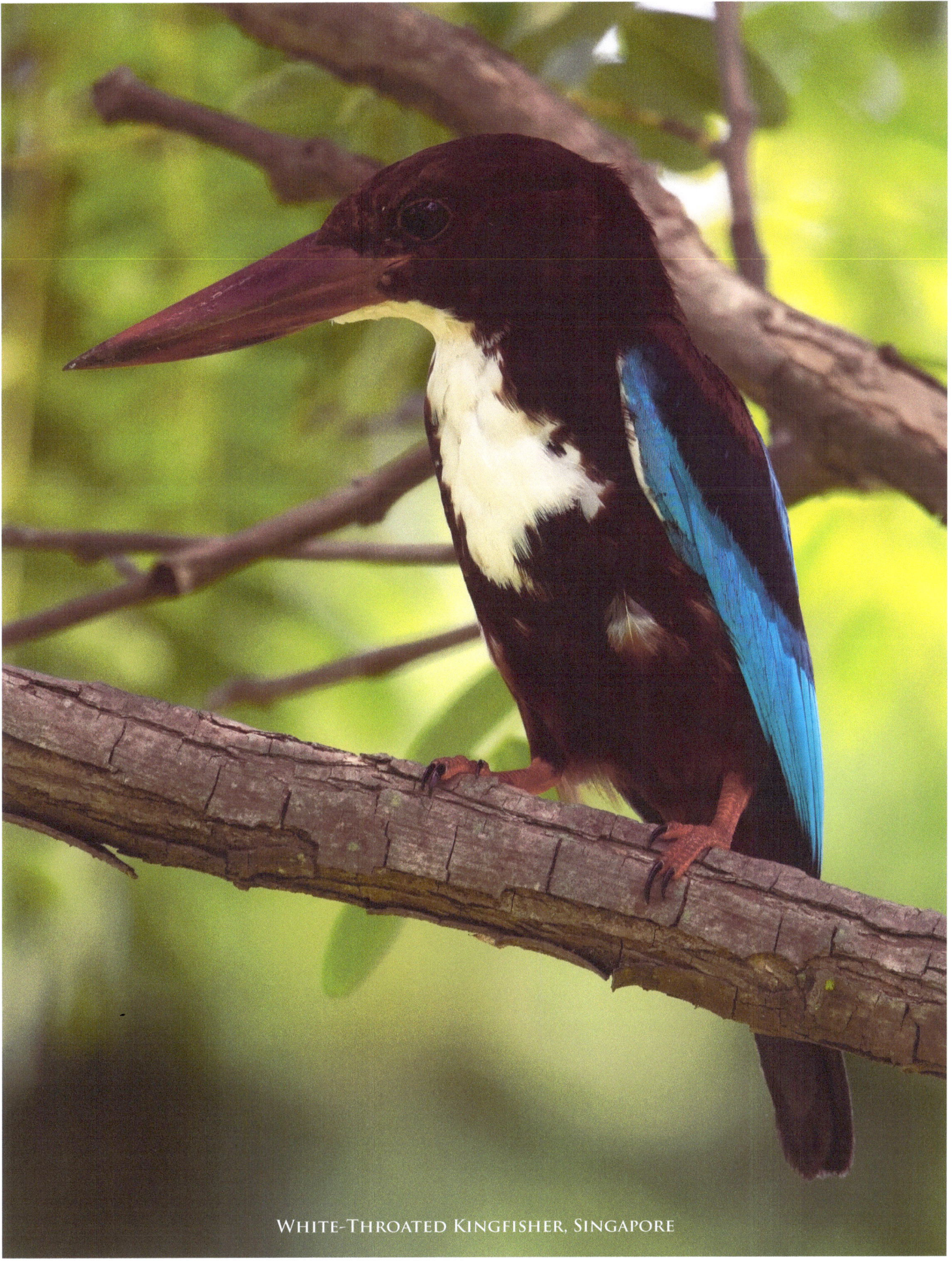

White-Throated Kingfisher, Singapore

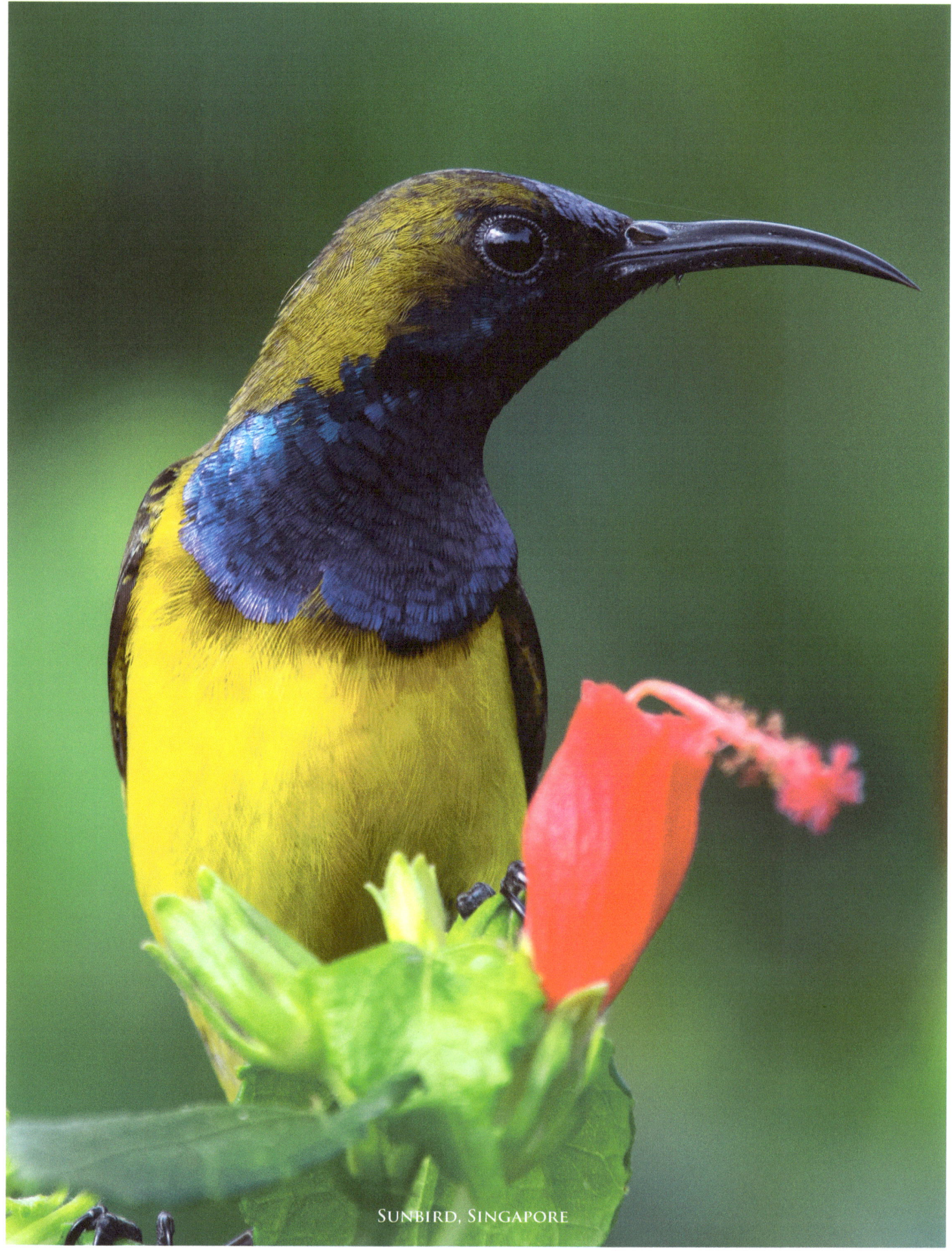

SUNBIRD, SINGAPORE

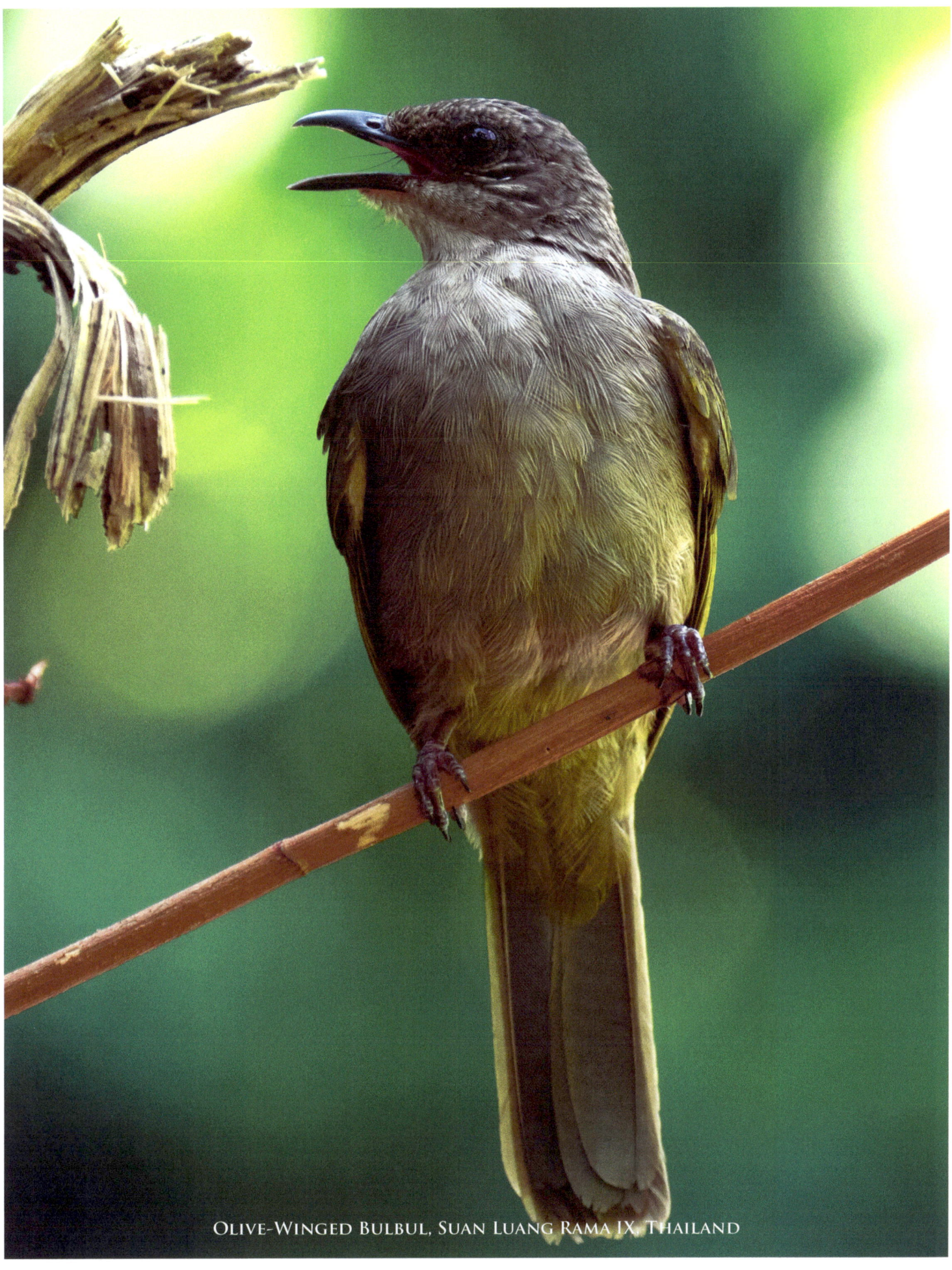

Olive-Winged Bulbul, Suan Luang Rama IX, Thailand

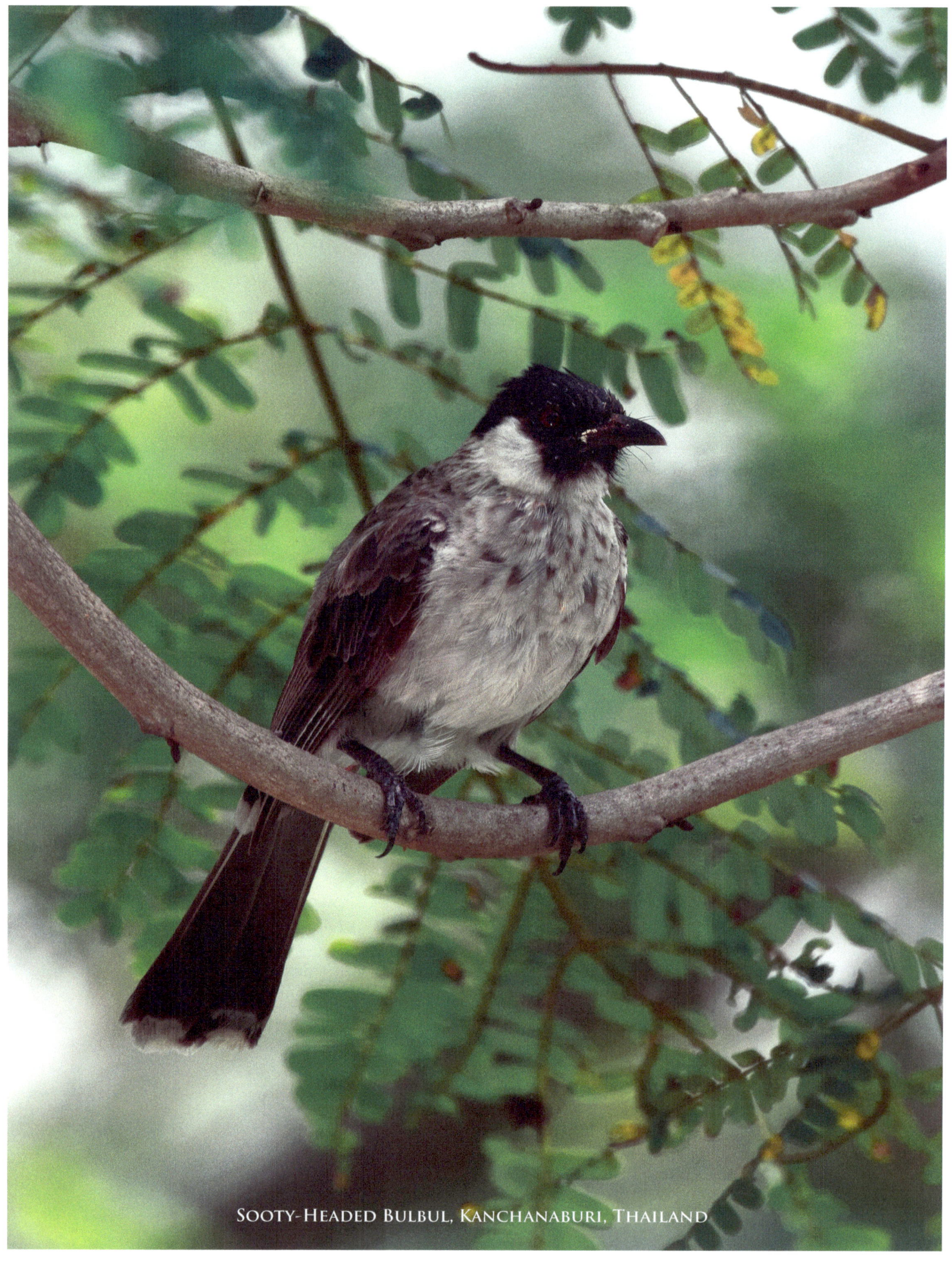

SOOTY-HEADED BULBUL, KANCHANABURI, THAILAND

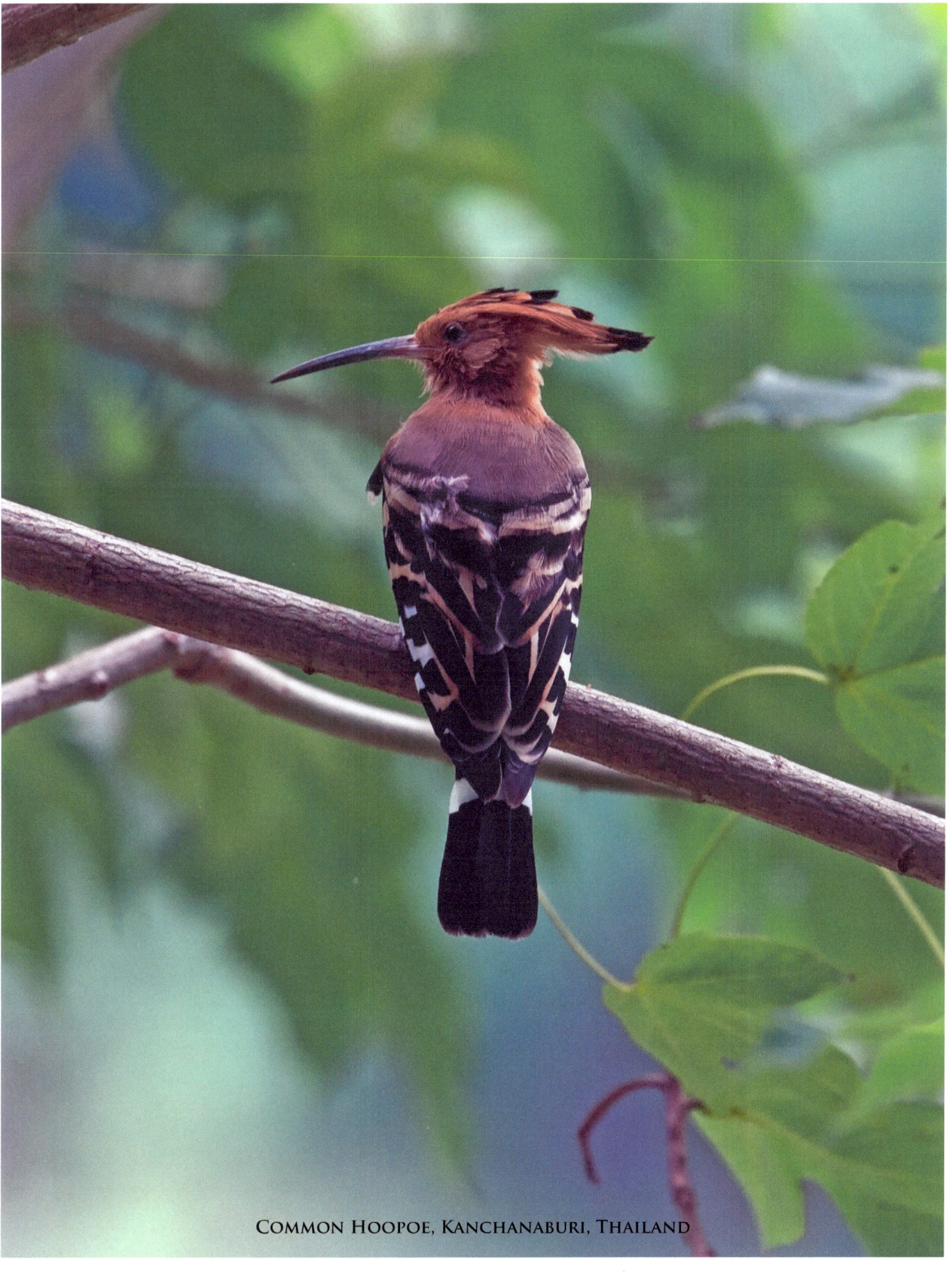

COMMON HOOPOE, KANCHANABURI, THAILAND

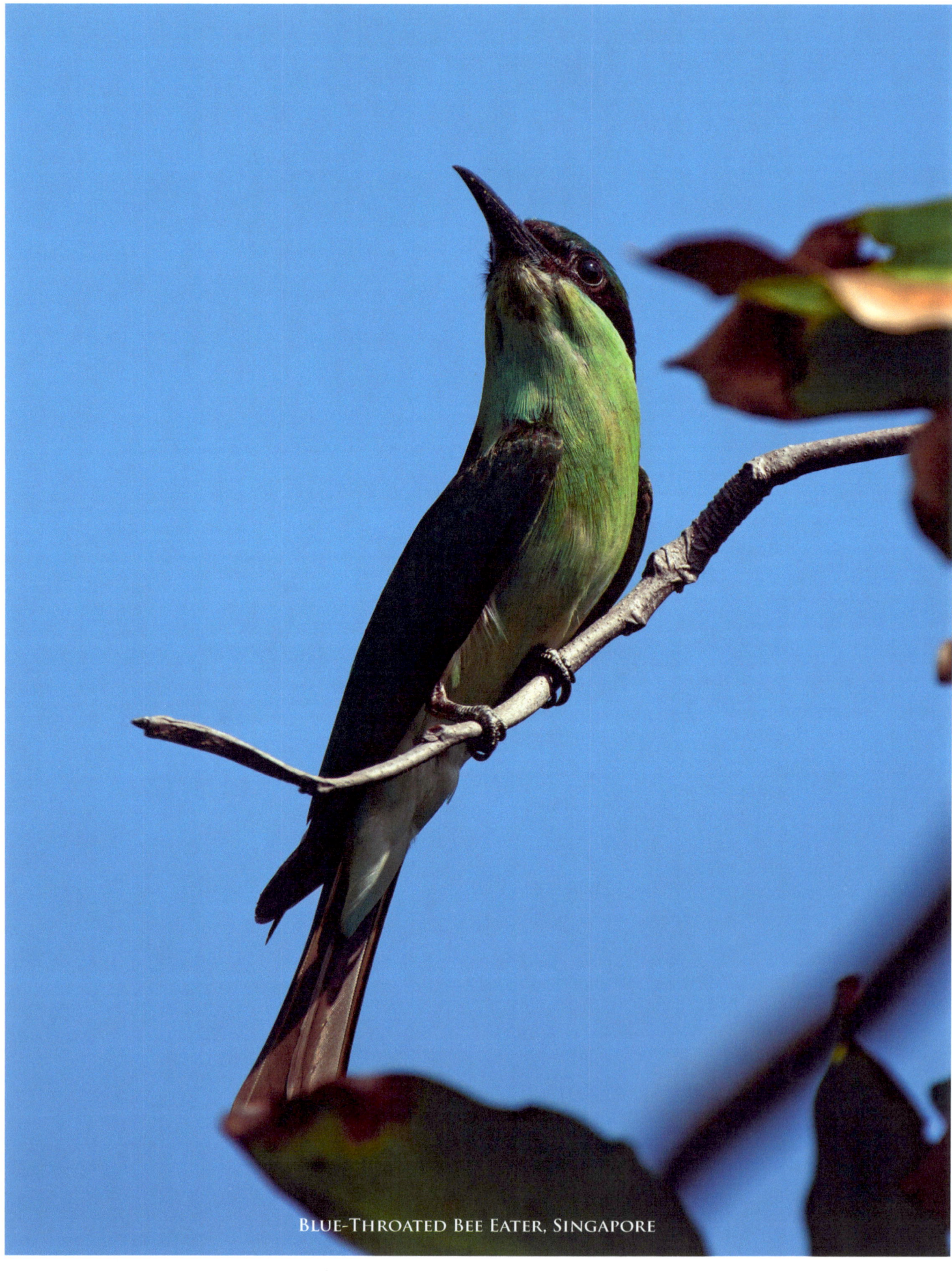

BLUE-THROATED BEE EATER, SINGAPORE

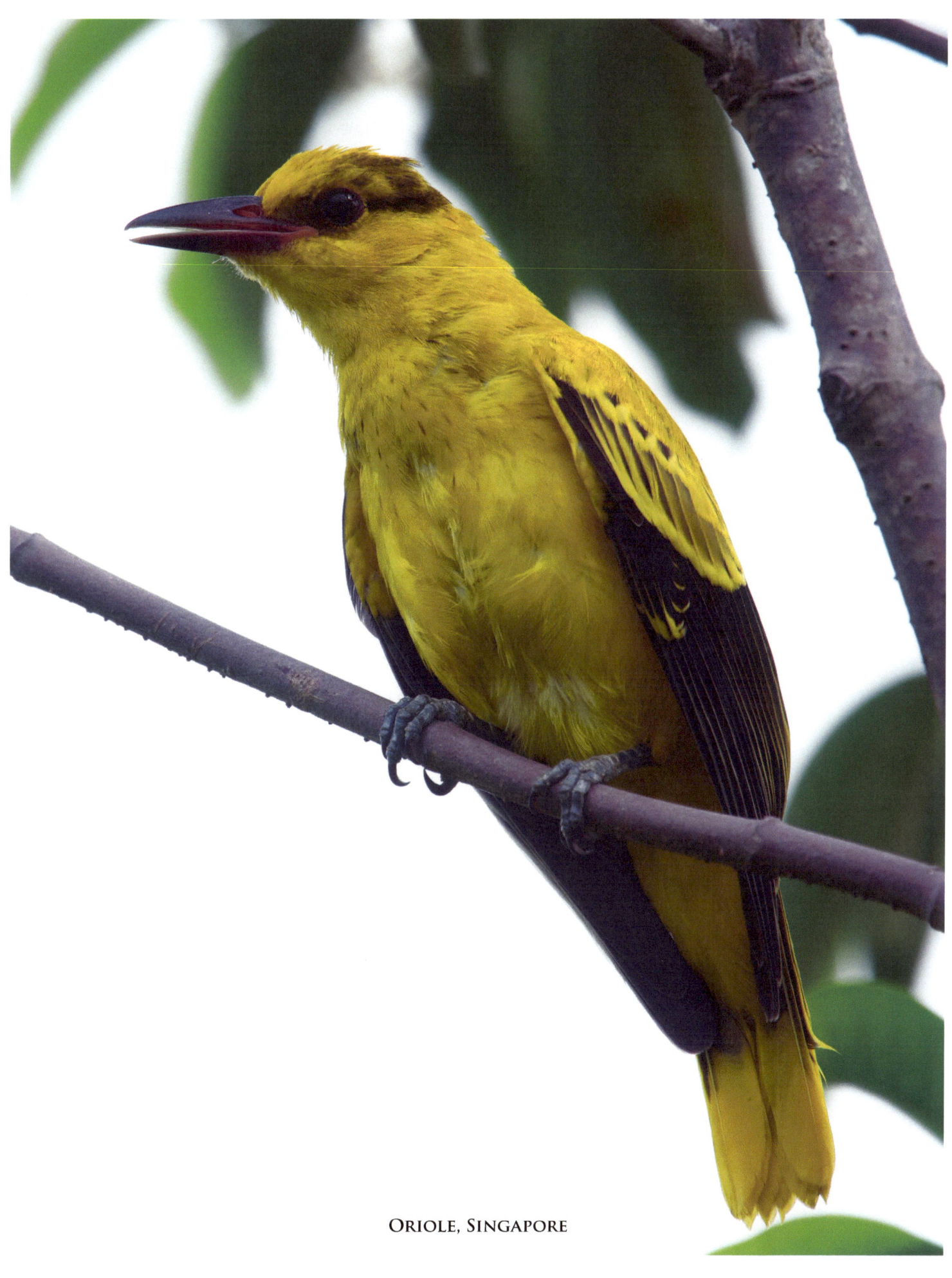

ORIOLE, SINGAPORE

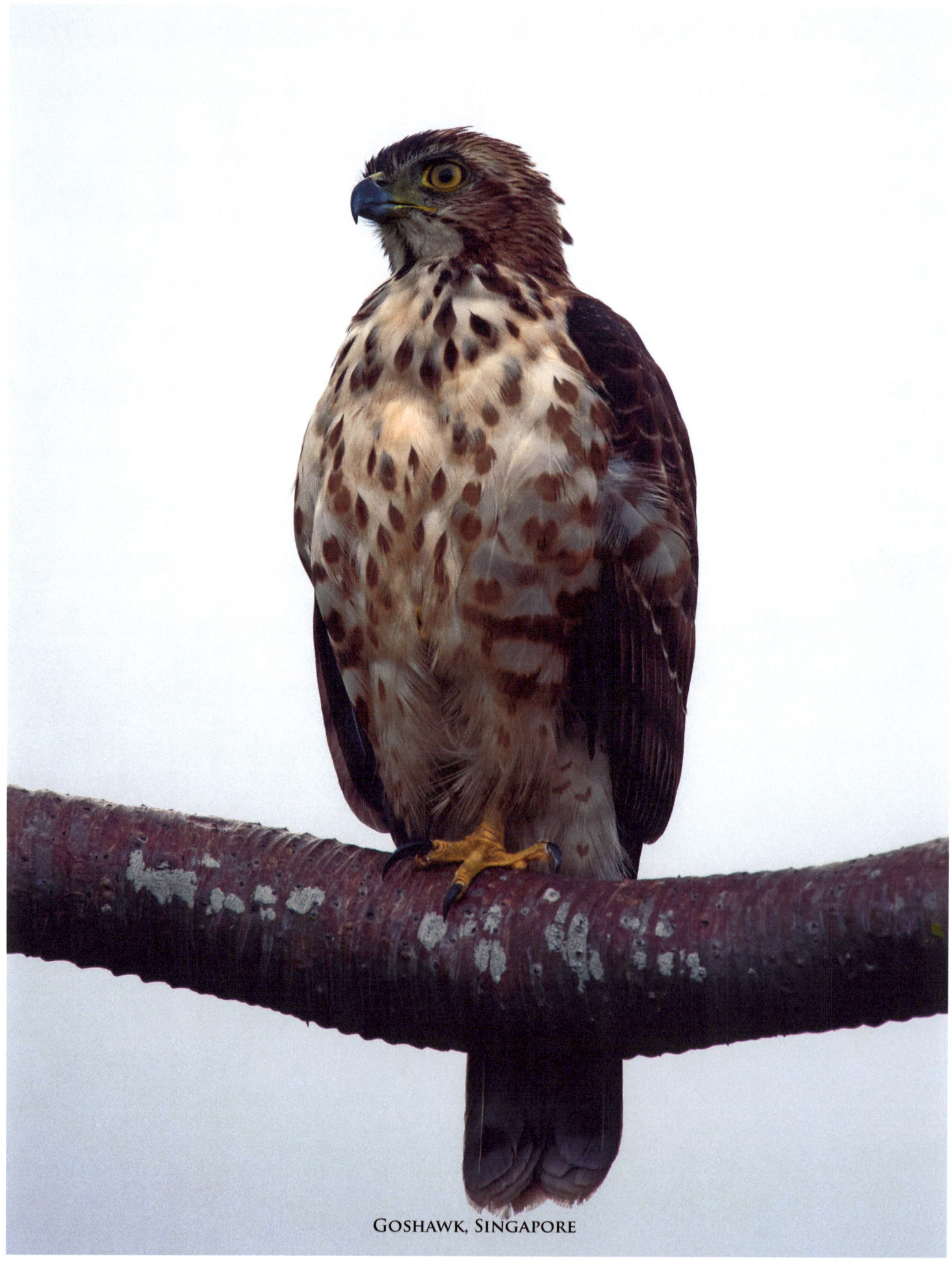

Goshawk, Singapore

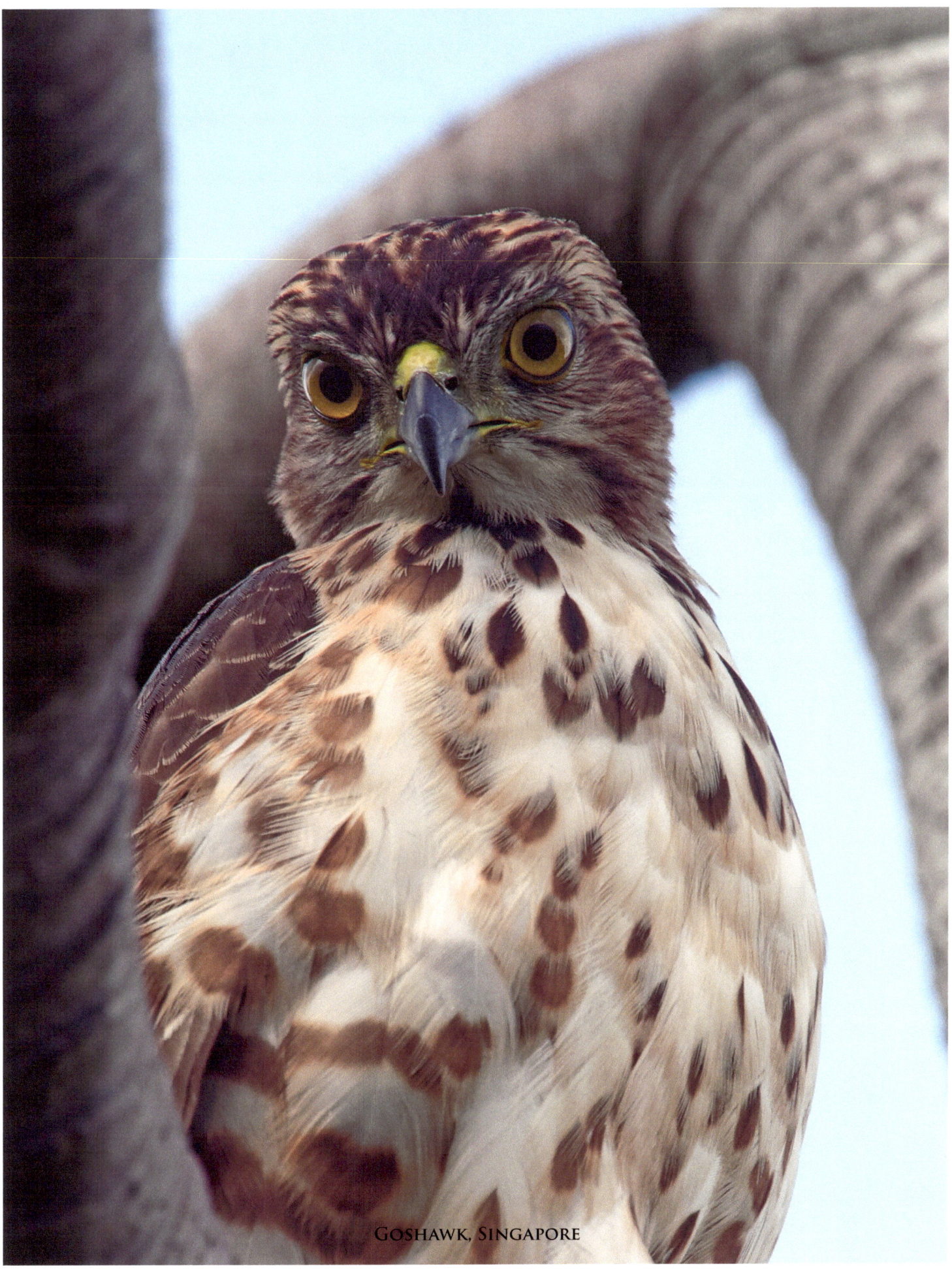

GOSHAWK, SINGAPORE

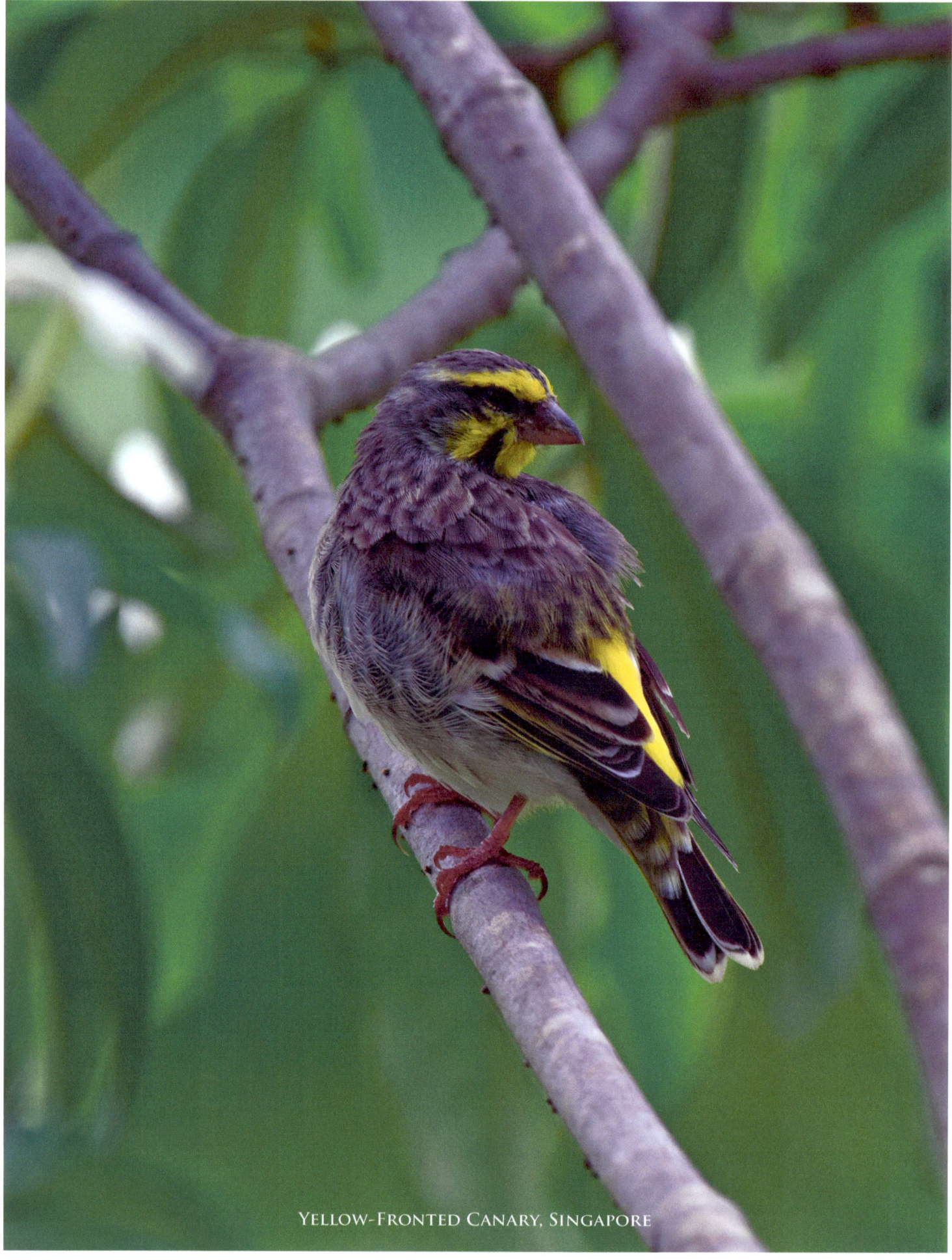

Yellow-Fronted Canary, Singapore

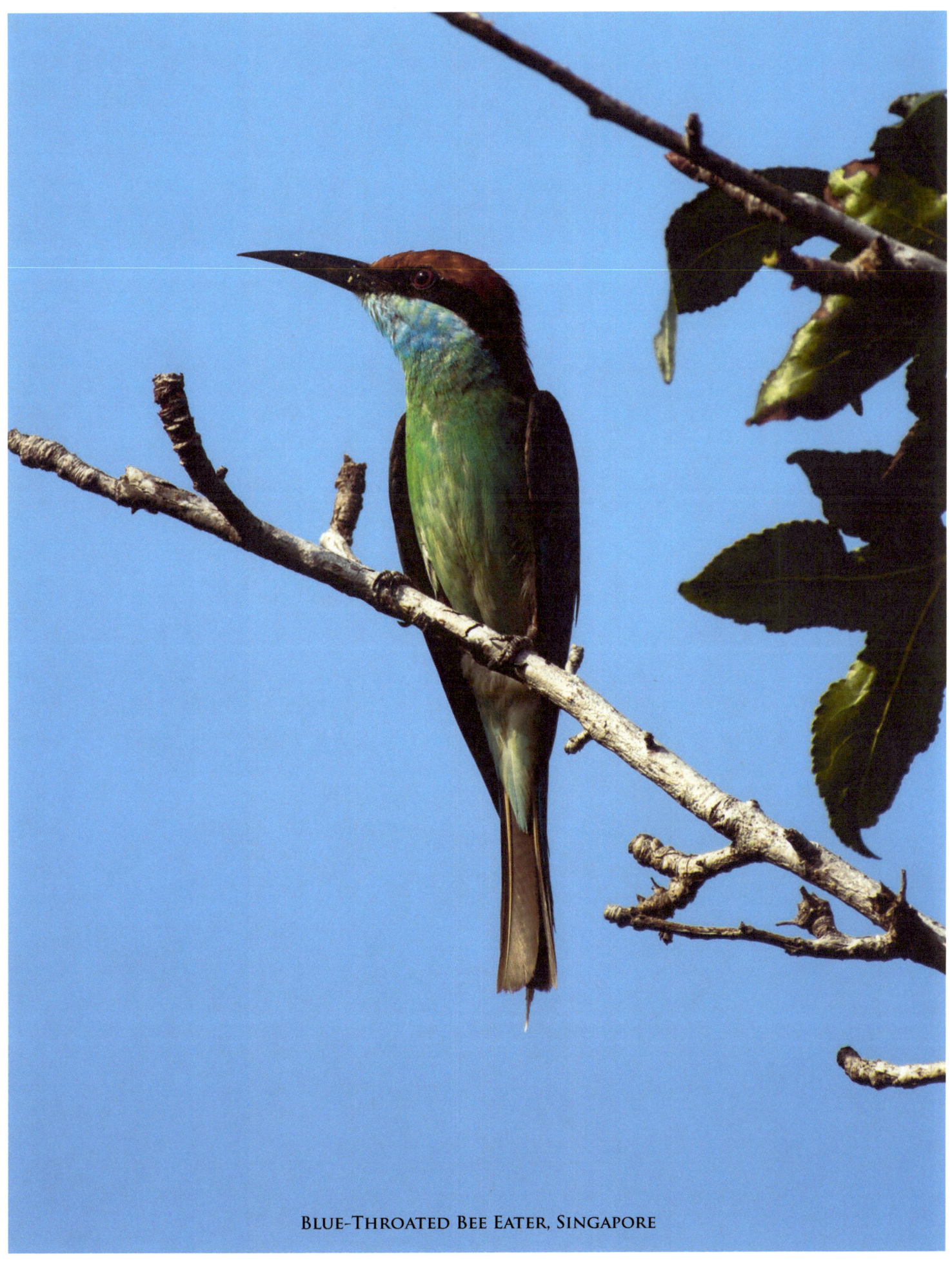

BLUE-THROATED BEE EATER, SINGAPORE

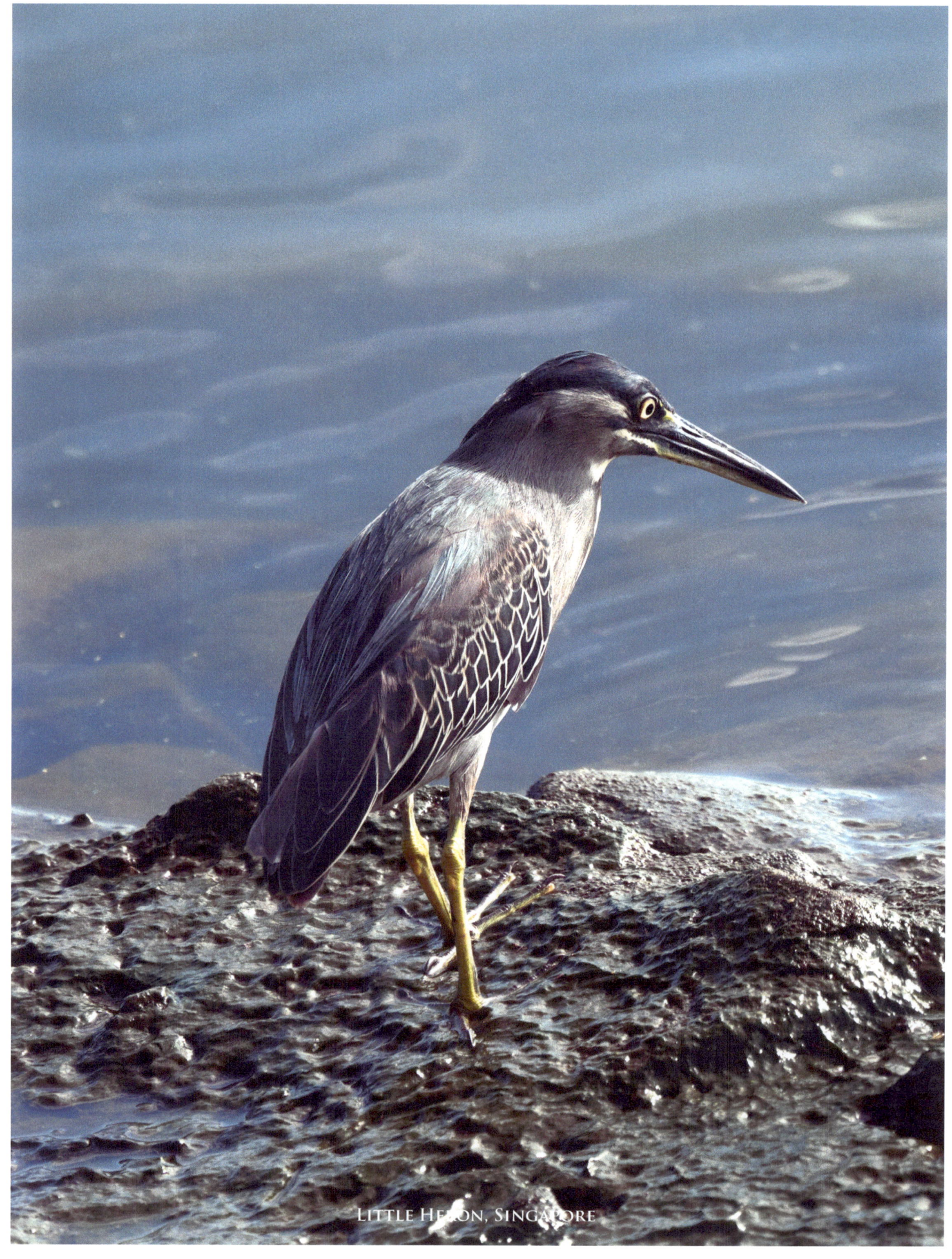

LITTLE HERON, SINGAPORE

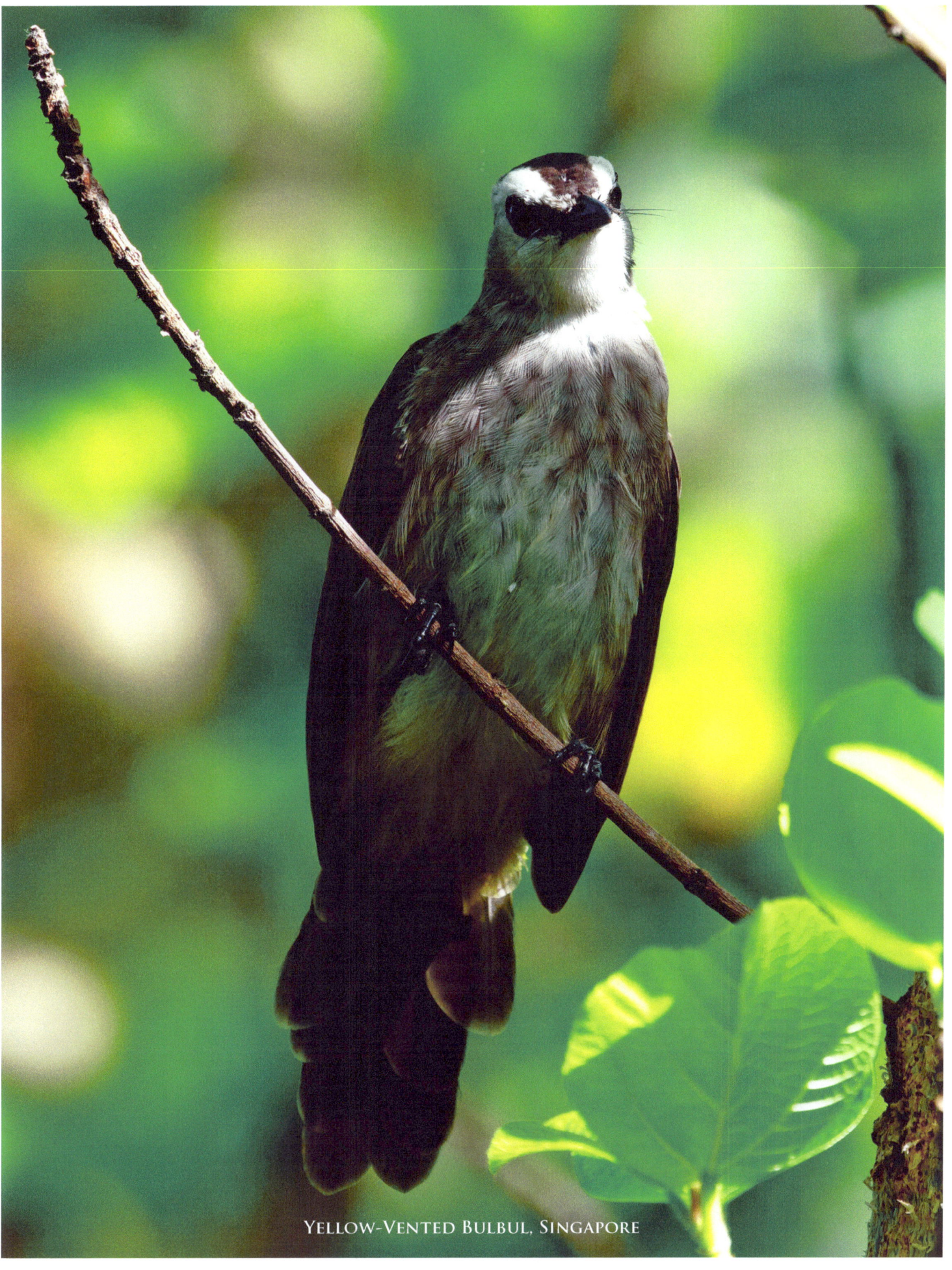

YELLOW-VENTED BULBUL, SINGAPORE

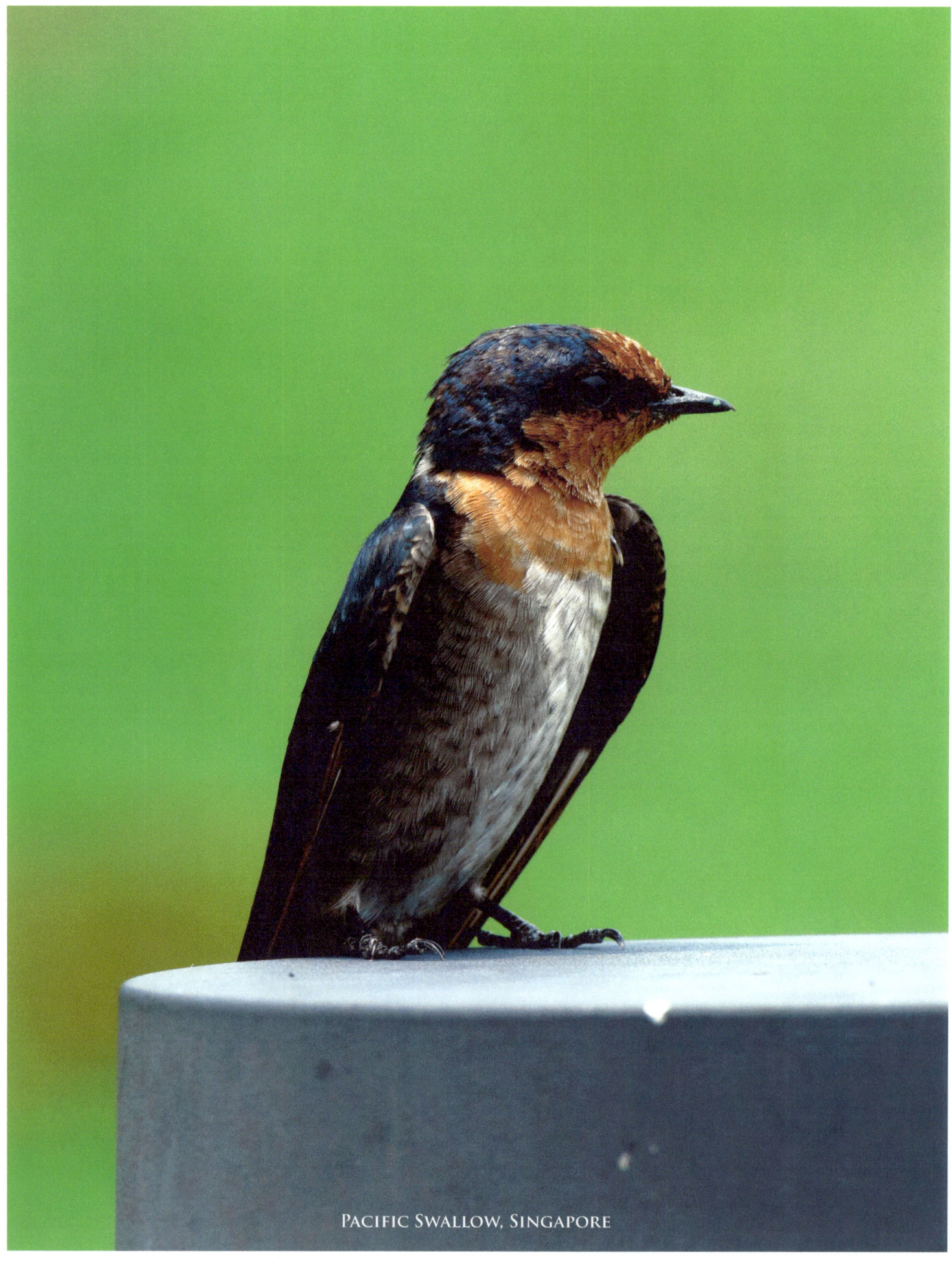

Pacific Swallow, Singapore

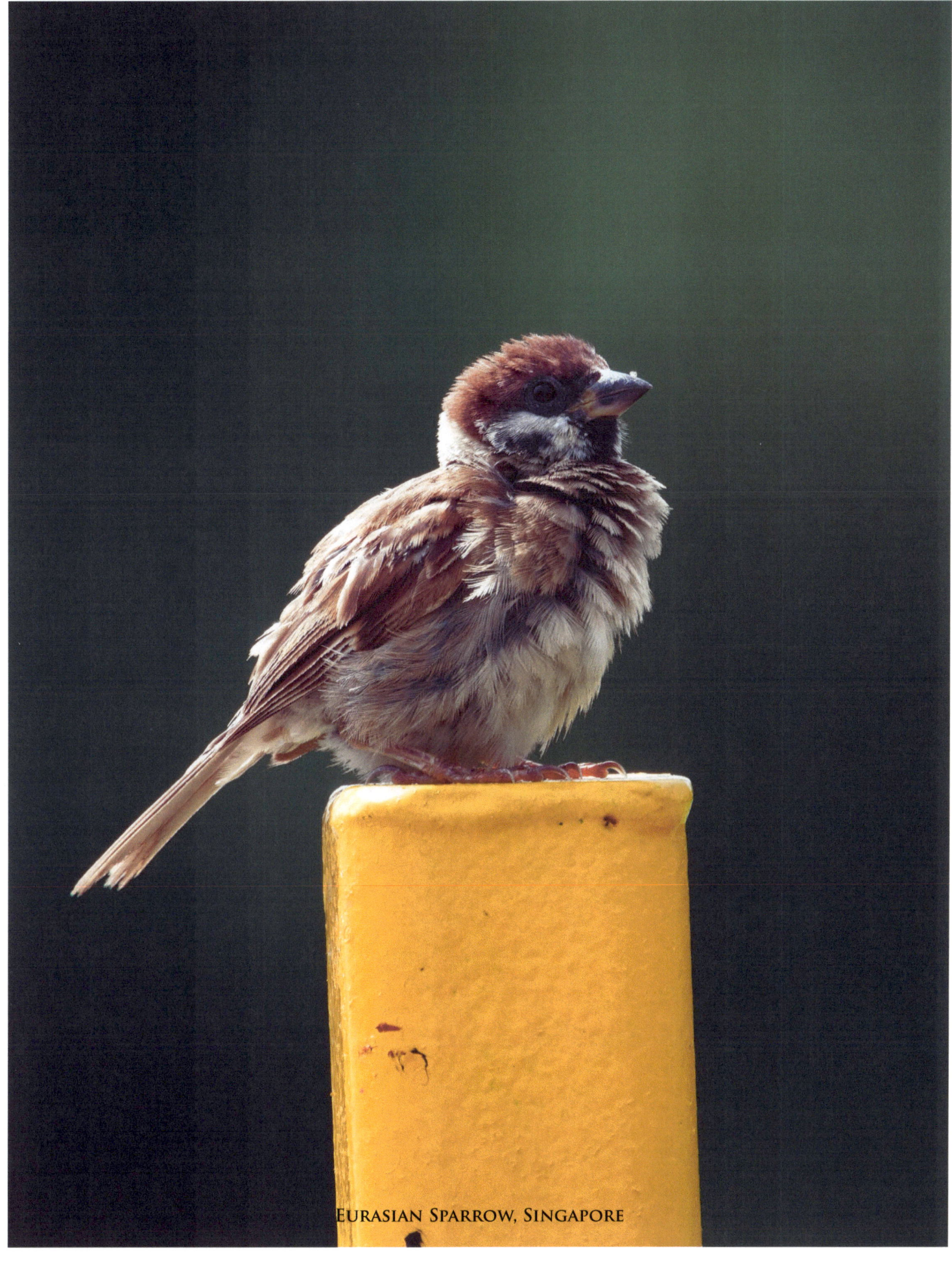

Eurasian Sparrow, Singapore

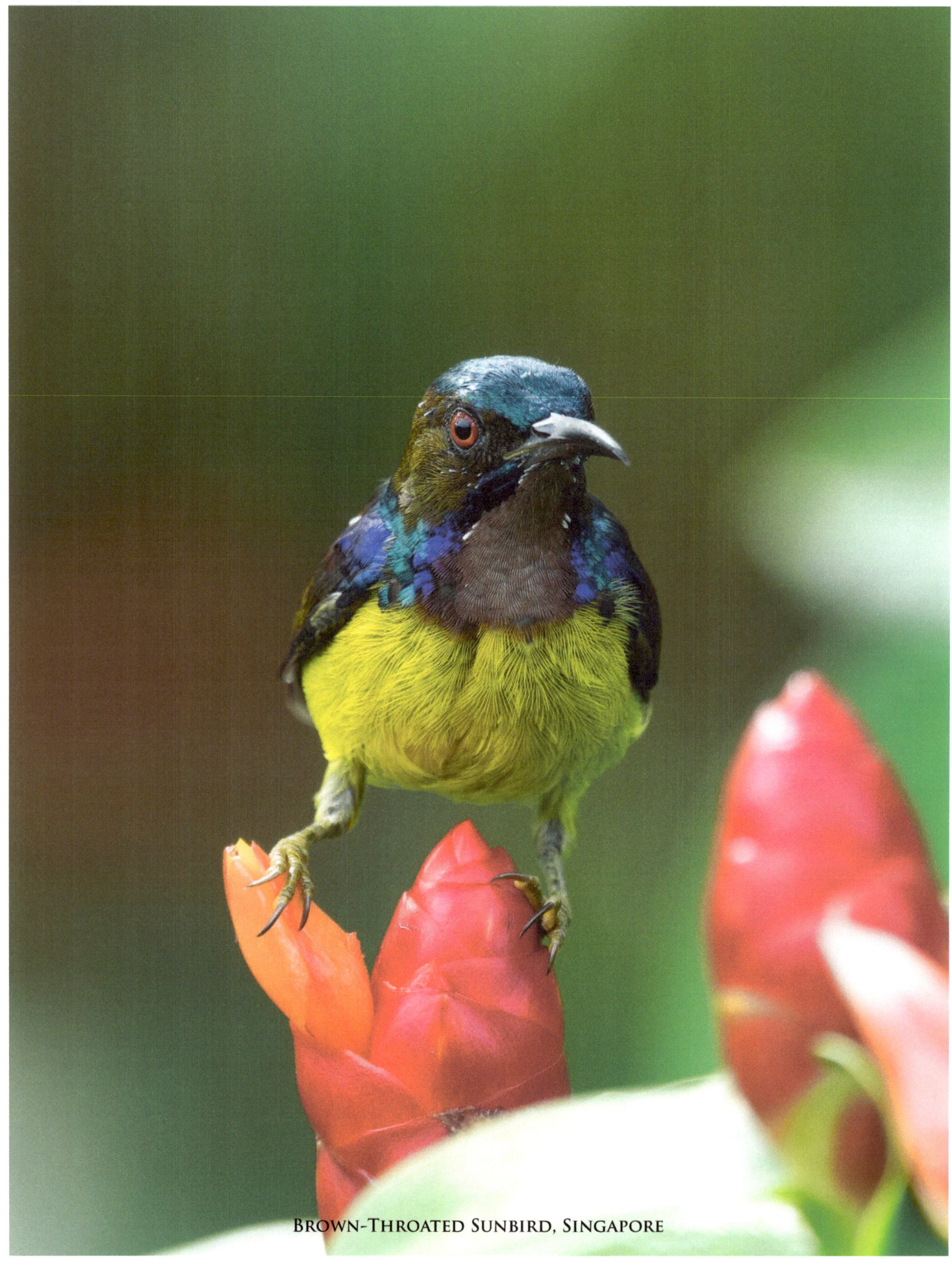

Brown-Throated Sunbird, Singapore

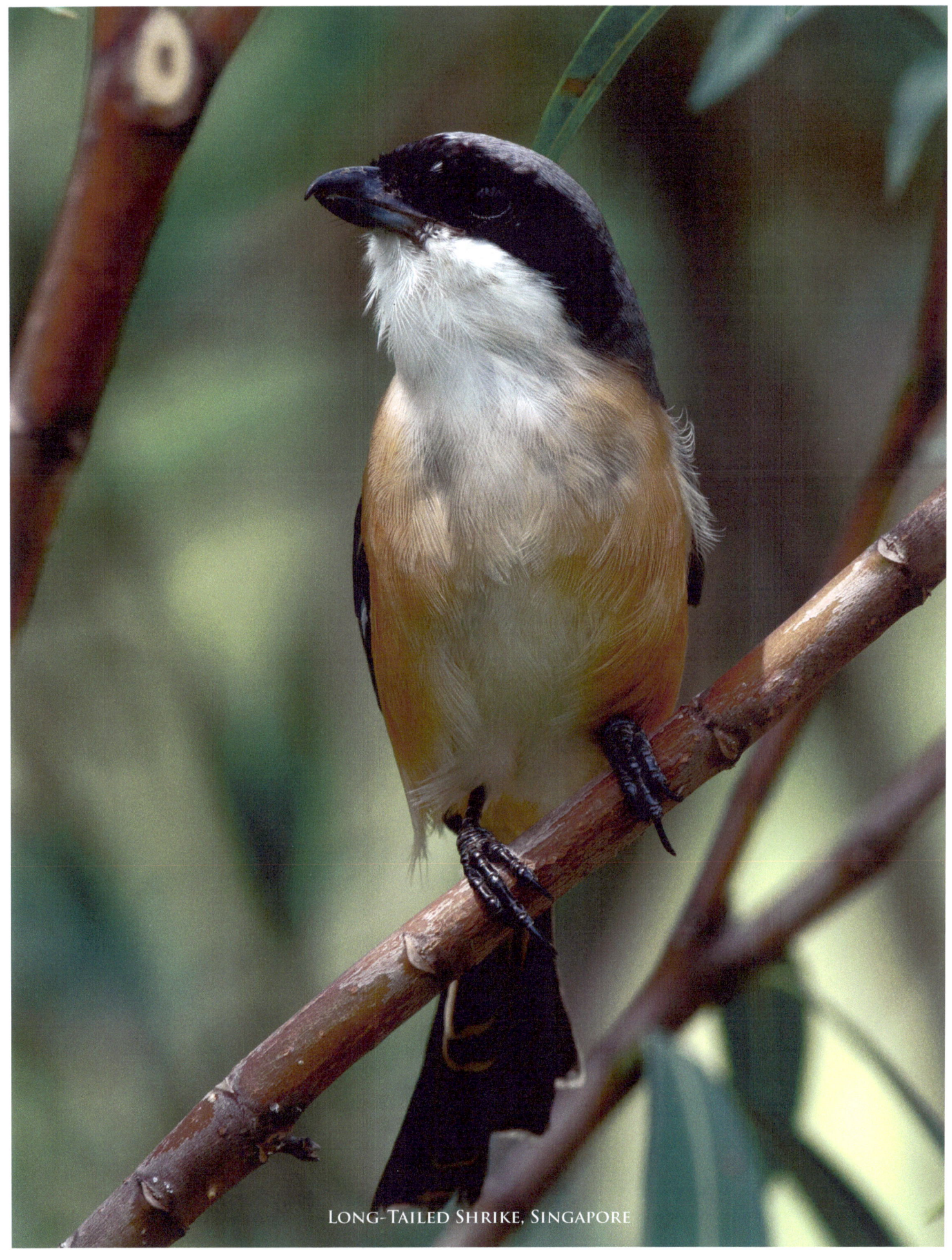

LONG-TAILED SHRIKE, SINGAPORE